Behind the Smile

Sex, Humor, and Terror

During the Glamour Years of Aviation

[signature]

By Bobbi Phelps Wolverton

A Flight Attendant's Journey

Published in the United States by Village Concepts, L.L.C.
First Edition.

Creative Nonfiction Disclaimer: All names are fictitious, except for celebrities and the late owner of World Airways, Ed Daly. Although the stories are true, the flight attendants are composites of several crew members. To aid in the narrative flow, timelines have been condensed.

Cover layout and design by Daryl Hunt.
Daryl's exceptional skills made my vision come alive.

Library of Congress Cataloging-in-Publication Data
    1. Wolverton, Barbara Phelps. 2. Flight attendant (1965-1973).
    3. Airplanes. 4. Travel: Vietnam – Europe – Orient – Southeast
Asia. 5. Author - American. 6. Memoir.

ISBN 978-0-615-82764-3 (alk. paper)

Visit the author's website at www.bobbiphelpswolverton.com

Cover photo: Bobbi and a Boeing 707 in Vietnam.
Back cover photo: Bobbi on the beach in Hawaii.

Dedication

To my sister, Ginny Phelps Clemens;
and my son, Matt Wolverton.

A special thanks to them. They read my stories
many, many times and encouraged me continuously.

And to my loving partner, Larry Chapman.
He was my business consultant who took care of me whenever I
isolated myself in the office. He made meals, fixed my computer, and
ran errands while I wrote and edited for weeks and months on end.

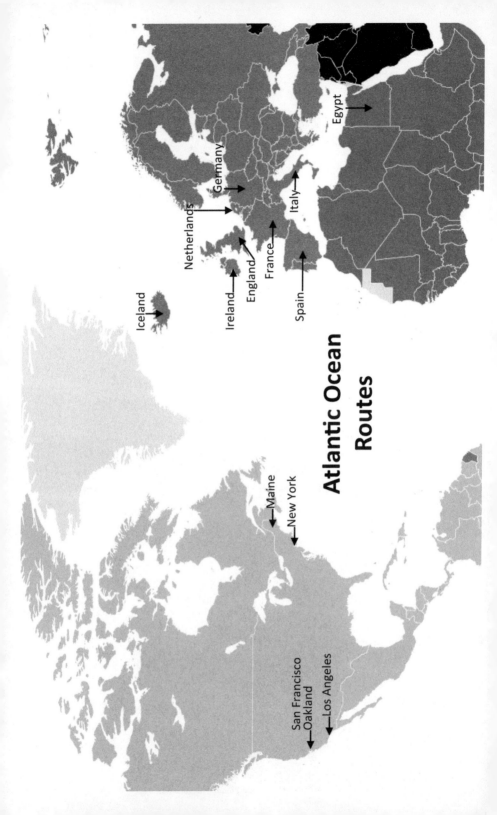

Atlantic Ocean Routes

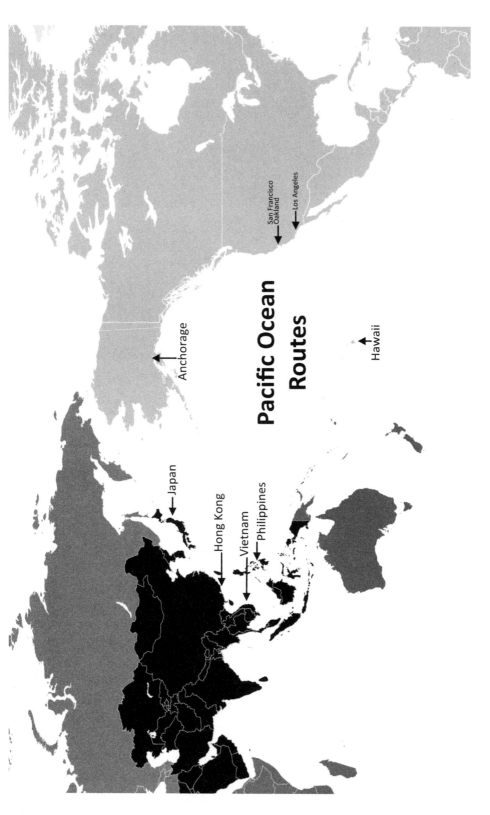

Pacific Ocean Routes

Anchorage

San Francisco
Oakland

Los Angeles

Hawaii

Japan

Hong Kong

Vietnam

Philippines

Table of Contents

Introduction:

THEN AND NOW

For most travelers today, flying is no longer special. Long lines at airports and crowded airplanes only add to a passenger's discomfort.

But flying wasn't always that way. As a young woman just out of college, I was fortunate to work as an international flight attendant (or stewardess, as we were then known) between 1965 and 1973, the glamour years of aviation.

Back then, flying was an exotic adventure, almost elitist. Fewer than 10% of Americans had ever flown. People dressed up for the occasion—men wore suits, and women wore dresses with gloves and high heels. Flight attendants sported designer uniforms and carried distinctly styled suitcases.

No movies were shown on board, and no connections for electronic gear existed. Airlines allowed smoking and even permitted cigars on special flights. The captain rarely locked his door and often agreed to cockpit visits.

As fares decreased more travelers took to planes, and today 90% of Americans have flown. We now live in an era of mass air transportation and flying is routine.

My time in the airline industry wasn't a planned career choice. Feeling stuck in a secretarial position and longing for adventure, I managed to secure an interview and passed the grueling four-week training. In many ways, flying was a dream career. I was paid a good salary and traveled the world. During my layovers in foreign countries, I saw much of Europe and the Orient and had incredible cultural experiences not available to the average tourist. But at the same time it was also hard, sometimes unGlamourous, and often dangerous work—both in the air and on the ground.

I learned to savor the joys and cope with the heartaches of flying, as I became a more confident woman. I performed my duties with skill and professionalism and never took my responsibilities for granted. I tasted the world's pleasures, made lasting friendships and memories, and finally earned by father's approval.

Enjoy *Behind the Smile*, an account of one woman's adventures during a more innocent and Glamourous time.

Bobbi Phelps Wolverton

Note: The stories in *Behind the Smile* apply to both World and Saturn Airways. Saturn was bought out by Trans International in 1976. World Airways is still in business.

FIRE!

Nervous passengers crammed the shaking aircraft. Thunder rumbled, streaks of lightning divided the dark skies, and a massive deluge poured from the clouds.

"Wow!" Janet said to me, nodding her head toward one of the jet's windows. "Look at that lightning!"

Violent winds rocked the airplane as we made our final approach to Los Angeles International Airport. A torrent of rain drenched the runway as our plane smacked down amid pools of water. I had been a flight attendant for less than a month when we landed late that night. I sat on the front jump seat, facing a crowded plane of anxious faces.

Suddenly I heard a loud bang. Was it thunder? *Was it the plane?*

Turning toward a window, I saw bright orange flames erupting from one of the engines. The blaze flared on the wet runway and seemed to be reaching for the plane's undercarriage. Raging fear overtook me.

I stood up and shouted, *"FIRE! FIRE!"*

The nearby passengers, already terrified by the thunderstorm and rough landing, stared at me in horror.

I rushed into the cockpit, and again yelled, "FIRE!"

Slamming the cockpit door behind me, I raced to the forward exit and grabbed the red handle, positioning myself to open the entrance door the instant the plane stopped. A chute would unfurl and the passengers would be able to slide down safely to the tarmac below.

Janet, the senior flight attendant, grabbed my shoulders and shoved me back onto the jump seat.

"Nothing is wrong!" she cried. "It's a reflection from the engines!"

Janet turned to the terrified passengers. "She's a brand-new flight attendant and still learning."

They listened to her polite explanation but continued to glare at me while gathering their belongings. I averted their eyes and lowered my head in humiliation.

"Thank you for flying with us," I mumbled softly as they tramped down the exit stairs, shaking their heads in dismay.

Once the passengers had deplaned, I hesitantly walked into the cockpit. I knew I faced termination. The flight crew ignored me, busy with their end-of-flight duties. As I began my apologies to the captain, the crew looked up and broke into smiles and laughter. The engines had merely backfired, or, in technical terms, a compressor stall was created by a strong, reverse thrust to the engines. In the darkness, the wet landing strip magnified the flames.

When we were alone, Captain Dean, a robust man in his late forties, gave me a stern lecture and said, "I suggest you study the emergency manual more carefully."

He put on his raincoat and secured the belt around his waist. He kindly patted me on the shoulder, descended the stairs to the tarmac, and marched ahead, his body bent into the wind. Demoralized, I followed the last crew members into the terminal, agonizing over my future with the airline. I was certain this was my last flight.

Captain Dean was a strict superior, but showed sympathy whenever he deemed it justified. He reported nothing to headquarters.

RED ON WHITE

Only a few weeks earlier, in January 1965, I worked my first trip as a flight attendant. Inspired by the prospects of an exciting new career, I couldn't sleep the night before. Although I had packed my luggage and ironed my uniform, my nails had not been polished.

On the way to the Oakland airport in my little MGA, I added coral gloss to my nails at every stoplight. While driving across the Bay Bridge, I draped my left hand out the car window to hasten the drying process. To dry the other hand, I awkwardly maneuvered my right hand across my chest and out the driver's window. It made for dangerous driving, but my nails finally dried. I arrived safely and parked proudly in the area designated *Crew Members Only*.

The cockpit and cabin crews had already convened at operations, the airline's coordinating center. We met in a dimly lit room, no larger than a small bedroom. The men stood before the office counter in their dark uniforms while the flight attendants, in beige uniforms and jockey-style hats, waited for the dispatcher.

"You'll fly to Anchorage," he told us. "After refueling, you'll continue to Tachikawa and layover for a couple of days."

I couldn't believe it. My first trip was a turnaround flight to Japan. I donned my leather gloves and signed in.

While waiting for final departing instructions, Ann, the senior flight attendant, checked our hair, makeup, and overall appearance. We wore three-inch heels and thigh-high stockings attached to clips inside tight girdles. Pantyhose had not yet been invented.

"Your hair needs to be shorter when you next report to work," she instructed Connie, a California recruit. "It can't touch your collar."

The other three flight attendants passed inspection. And so did I—that is, until Ann asked me to remove my leather gloves.

"What a mess!" she gasped.

The nail polish had stuck to the inside of my gloves, forming a gooey, coral smear over each fingernail. Ann gave me "the look" and solved the problem with quick strokes from her polish remover.

"You must allow more time for personal chores," she cautioned, but allowed me to fly without polish.

Next, Ann tested our knowledge about medical and emergency procedures. We then went outside and boarded a long black limousine. There were nine of us: the captain, first officer, engineer, navigator, and one senior and four junior flight attendants. Our chauffeur drove us an hour north to Travis Air Force Base. We were flying U.S. troops on the first leg of their flight to Vietnam. During the Vietnam War, our government enlisted all U.S. international airlines, both charter and scheduled companies, to transport troops and equipment to and from South Vietnam.

I could barely contain my excitement and talked nonstop with Connie during the drive north. We had both graduated from airline school the week before and were thrilled to be working a flight to the Orient.

Outside the Travis terminal we boarded our Boeing 707, removed our hats and coats, and began our pre-flight duties. Ann approved paperwork and coordinated cabin responsibilities. The two galley attendants verified that the correct amount of meals, tray set-ups, and beverages had been boarded.

Connie and I were assigned to the cabin. After checking supplies in the lavatories, we confirmed the placement of all safety equipment. Oxygen bottles and fire extinguishers had to be full and fastened securely in the overhead compartments.

Each passenger seat and jump seat had a life vest underneath it. We had to bend over and physically touch every vest in the airplane as part of our check-in duties. With almost two hundred passengers, our waists stayed trim and toned by regularly performing this awkward but required task.

An hour later Navy personnel started to board. Since this was a charter flight, the cabin had been configured into one compartment, military class only. I remained in the aisle, handing out pillows and blankets.

Over the PA system came the announcement, "Prepare for departure."

With these words, the captain notified the flight attendants to close and lock all cabinets and to arm the exits. The plane began its backward movement.

Connie and I demonstrated life vests, oxygen masks, and emergency exit functions. I noticed how handsome the sailors looked in their starched, white uniforms. They stared and smiled at me. I felt conspicuous, yet delighted by their attention. Being a flight attendant was going to be fabulous.

After the demo, Connie took her seat near the aft, right-hand, window exit. I walked to the rear jump seat, double-checking seat belt compliance along the way, and sat next to Susan.

We listened to the roar of the engines while we sat in the gray, cavernous area by the aft exit door. As the plane raced down the runway, I felt an unbelievable rush, an exhilarating high, as my body was thrust hard against the seat back.

The moment the plane lifted off the ground, I punched the air with my fist and cried, "Yes!"

"I made it," I excitedly said to Susan. "I'm now official, and I'm flying to Japan!"

As we continued our upward climb, Susan brought me back to reality and told me what I should expect during the next few hours.

"Once the no-smoking sign is switched off, you'll put on your apron and assist me in serving juice."

Susan secured a portable counter across the front of the galley—a small stainless steel kitchen complete with four mini-ovens and numerous cabinets. She turned on the ovens, all previously loaded with meals from the catering contractor.

While Susan prepared the galley and poured tomato juice into paper cups, Connie and I placed the cups on plastic trays. We began to serve juice to those seated in the back two-thirds of the plane.

In 1965 aisle carts had not been invented and Boeing 707 jets did not have enhanced stabilizers. While I delivered trays of juice to the waiting sailors, the plane swayed and bounced and I was unsteady on my feet. I had not yet acquired my "air legs."

Many of those beautiful boys received bright drops of tomato juice on their clean, white uniforms. They raised their hands in protest whenever I approached. Much to their chagrin, I remained in the aisle most of the flight.

A dinner course came next. From the rear galley, Connie and I carried two heavy trays in front of us, one above the other. Each tray held a hot entree and two vegetables, a roll and dessert, metal flatware, and two beverage mugs.

The smell of brewing coffee drifted through the cabin. Once the meal service ended, we filled coffee cups and retrieved dirty trays. Before long the sailors were fast asleep and I was exhausted. I felt like I had walked the entire flight to Anchorage.

When we refueled and resumed our journey to Japan, we began the chores again: another snack and meal service, drink distribution, tray pickup, and galley cleaning. We inspected the lavatories for supplies and routinely checked the passengers.

"The flight attendants will pass out Japanese immigration and customs forms," Ann announced over the PA system. "Please fill them out before you enter the terminal. If you need help, ask the girls for assistance."

Susan, Connie, and I instructed the passengers and even filled out some of the forms for their signatures. Most had never been on an airplane, and none had ever been to Japan.

Before long we heard the "ping" of the no-smoking sign being illuminated, the signal for us to sit down and prepare for landing.

Parked next to each other on the rear jump seat, Susan and I counted the steps I had taken since we left California. We figured I had walked up and down the aisle 164 times. No wonder I was beat.

While taxiing to the terminal we switched to high heels and put on our hats and coats. Once the plane stopped, I stood at the bottom of the rear ramp and apologized to the men in red-dotted uniforms, wishing them all "good luck."

After a quick check of the cabin, the crew walked into the Tachikawa airport and we retrieved our suitcases, passed through customs, and left the military terminal. By the time we reached the waiting limousine, we had been on duty eighteen hours and would clock another hour before arriving at our hotel rooms.

I slumped into the leather seat and leaned back, recalling the time in airline school when I thought a flight attendant's life was Glamourous.

What was I thinking? How did I end up here?

CALIFORNIA BOUND

My unexpected career in the airline industry resulted from a series of mishaps that started in 1964 at the age of twenty-two. Using my hard-earned babysitting and lawn-mowing money, I purchased a black, 1959 MGA convertible. I had graduated from college and secretarial school, and was now looking for adventure.

"I want to drive to San Francisco," I informed my parents.

As an unconventional student of life, my mother thought a trip from Connecticut to the West Coast was reasonable, but she wanted a few assurances.

My father had a different point of view: "I think your idea is ridiculous. No job and driving by yourself across country? No, you do not have my permission."

My mother encouraged her children to explore, to question, and to dream big. My father lived in a straitjacket of traditional conformity. Throughout my life, I benefited from dad's strict boundaries and mom's eccentric support.

Soon after our California discussion, mom found

a secretarial position for me at the Pan Am office in San Francisco. Our neighbors knew a student who needed transportation to Sacramento. Fred Gannon, an under-graduate at Stanford University, agreed to pay half the auto expenses.

My dad relented, although he still objected to my traveling with an unknown man. On the day of departure he roped my suitcase to the MGA's trunk rack and insisted I call each evening. Mom had confirmed four overnights across the country with friends and relatives.

Beginning the California journey in my MGA.

When I picked up Fred in Pennsylvania, he stood a skinny six-feet tall and wore an oversized suit. His black-framed glasses accented his pale, pockmarked face. Not exactly the California beach boy I had expected. When I telephoned my parents that first night from my sister's home in Chicago, my description of Fred seemed to ease my father's worries.

The next morning we drove to Des Moines. Because the MGA did not have a heater, air blew from the engine and warmed the car's interior. In winter, the hot air was a blessing. In other seasons the floorboards sizzled and my feet baked. That summer day the air was stifling. I shed my shoes and drove barefoot.

After stopping for gas, I changed to the passenger seat. Fred shifted to the driver's position and off we went. About an hour later, I asked him to pass me my shoes.

"Didn't you see them?" he asked. "I put them next to the gas pumps when we filled up."

"No, of course I didn't see them."

He had left my shoes at a gas station! I was furious. They were brand new loafers, and I had saved a whole month to buy them. The shoe episode initiated my distaste for Fred. Each evening I peppered my parents with travel updates. Dad loved every negative comment about Fred's behavior.

A massive thunderstorm hit us when we reached Kansas. Strong winds forced a gap between the front window frame and the convertible top. After being splashed by numerous passing vehicles, Fred became upset and I resumed driving.

When we reached Colorado, Fred returned to driving. The rain had ceased and we could see snow-capped mountains in the distance. As we drove past Denver, Fred fiddled with the clutch and grated the gears. After listening to the grinding for the umpteenth time, I snarled, "Move over. I'll drive."

With built-up anger, I drove the next sixteen hours on sheer adrenaline to his Sacramento home. After napping in the family's den, I retraced my route to the freeway and drove in delightful solitude to the *City by the Bay*, San Francisco.

California's speed limit on the interstate had been sixty miles per hour. The speed limit dropped to fifty on the Bay Bridge, but I never noticed the change.

A policeman drove up behind me, clocking my excessive speed. As I moved to the passing lane, a powerful gust of wind blew across the bridge. In an instant the convertible top ripped off and flew backwards, blanketing the front window of the patrol car.

I slammed on my brakes and pulled over to the side. In doing so, I cut off the officer who was now blinded by the convertible top. He pounded his brakes and barely missed rear-ending my car.

In the side mirror I saw a red-faced officer charging toward me, my convertible cover in his hands. He raged with anger as he reached for the door handle. But MGAs do not have outside handles, which enraged him even more.

"Open your goddamn door," he yelled. "Now!"

I released the inside latch and apologized for the flying top. He continued to bellow at me and produced a ticket book. Being extremely tired, I burst into tears.

The patrolman responded with compassion. While I explained my cross-country ordeal, he secured the wayward top. The rivet attachments had broken; my car had now become a nonfunctioning convertible. The officer delivered a strict sermon, but put away his ticket book. He pointed to nearby hotels and I checked into the one he suggested.

The next day I drove to the Pan Am office to begin the secretarial post that had been promised me back in Connecticut. During the past week the position had inadvertently been filled and I was told to wait for a future opening.

"But not to worry," the personnel director said. "We have a flight attendant position you can fill right now."

"Thanks," I said, "I'd rather wait."

With a college degree and secretarial training, I felt too qualified. My strict father had a poor impression of flight attendants. He assumed they were promiscuous, and I was too immature to fight his prejudices.

I left the Pan Am office and searched for work. The only available jobs were for unskilled workers. Disillusioned, I returned to my hotel room and counted money. I could no longer stay there without additional funds.

The following morning I drove to the YWCA. At the front desk lines of women were checking in and out. When it was my turn, I asked about the rates and requested a room.

The attendant answered, "You're out of luck. I·just rented the last one."

Finding myself in a strange city with no friends, no job, and no lodging, I was devastated. I returned to my open convertible, leaned on the steering wheel, and began to cry.

Just then, two young women approached. Carole Krohl and Barbara Wysocki, college graduates from Michigan, had just checked out of the "Y" and had overheard my conversation with the receptionist.

Carole introduced herself and said, "Can we help? We have an empty bedroom. A friend of ours won't be arriving for another three months."

Not knowing Carole or Barbara but having no other options, I readily agreed and followed them to Twin Peaks. Their furnished unit had two bedrooms and two bathrooms. In less than an hour I had gone from being homeless to living in a beautiful apartment overlooking the skyline of San Francisco.

Now I had a place to stay but still no income. Each day I inquired about available or upcoming secretarial positions. After a week of searching I became frustrated by the lack of quality jobs. I decided to protest.

The next day I drove to City Hall, an imposing building located on two square blocks. On entering I noticed a bulletin board with George Christopher listed as mayor. I intended to complain to him about San Francisco's job situation.

In my innocence, I didn't know that big city mayors do not have time for casual walk-ins. Luckily, Mayor Christopher was out of town. His assistant, Mr. Quinn, greeted me.

"Mayor Christopher met my father in New York," I informed Mr. Quinn. "He told dad that if I ever reached San Francisco, he would help me get a job."

That was a lie. They had never met, but they could have, and I was desperate.

Mr. Quinn invited me to meet Mrs. Wilkerson, manager of the secretarial pool. She inquired about my typing and shorthand skills and wondered about a possible start date.

"I can begin tomorrow," I replied.

Being in the secretarial pool provided me with a decent income and a chance to explore San Francisco. A few months later I met and dated Bob Benson, an attorney at a downtown law firm. But soon I craved adventure and no longer wanted to endure the monotony of daily commuting.

Bob suggested I check out World Airways, an international airline company located across the Bay in Oakland. His former girlfriend had worked there, and had enjoyed being paid to travel the Orient and Europe.

"That's my answer," I thought and applied that next morning.

THE INTERVIEW

"Are there any flight attendant positions still open?" I asked over the phone.

"Yes, a few. Classes start next week," the receptionist answered.

Since I inquired about employment, she bombarded me with questions.

"How old are you? Are you married? Do you wear glasses? How tall are you? What's your weight?"

During the 1960s, strict criteria were enforced if you wanted to become a flight attendant. One could not be married or wear eyeglasses. An attendant could not weigh over one hundred thirty-five pounds, and her weight had to be proportionate to her height (between five foot two and five foot eight). At the time I applied, my age had to be between twenty-one and twenty-eight.

Once I qualified in all five categories, she arranged an appointment for me with the chief flight attendant.

"Come in tomorrow at three p.m."

So many young women clamored to be flight attendants. Despite my father's reservations, I was pleasantly pleased to have obtained an interview. I no longer wanted a nine-to-five job, nor did I want to bring home the hassles of a secretarial profession. I wanted to be paid to travel the world, to have flexible hours with many days off, and to work in a Glamourous occupation.

"Who wouldn't?" I thought.

Besides physical qualifications, one was supposed to have a language or nursing background and some college education. These standards were ignored if the applicant had special attributes. A beauty queen or model might be accepted without meeting all the requirements.

On Wednesday, I parked my MGA in the lot at World's headquarters near the Oakland airport. I wore a navy suit and had my hair done in a bouffant flip, very popular at the time.

The airline office looked similar to others in the building -- with fake wall paneling and fluorescent lights. Miss Harris, the receptionist, looked up from her gray metal desk and introduced herself.

"You'll need to fill out these forms."

She gave me a clipboard with a pen and pointed to a desk I could use. I completed four pages of personal information and passed them back. She glanced at the forms and said, "Follow me" as she walked around her desk and placed the pages back in my hands.

Miss Harris escorted me down a dark hallway to the chief flight attendant's office. Diane Taylor stood as I entered and shook my hand. She was in her thirties, attractive, and immediately intimidating. Dressed in a tailored skirt, she wore a crisp white blouse and a bright scarf. Miss Taylor invited me to sit down, gesturing to a chair on the opposite side of her desk.

While I looked past her to the window outside, she read my paperwork. With an authoritative tone, she asked me to expand on my answers.

"How many languages do you know?" she asked.

"Five," I replied.

Apparently impressed by this response, Ms. Taylor never asked a follow-up question. In truth, I did know five languages. Aside from English, I had Spanish in high school and French in college. I also had a Japanese pen pal in third grade who translated a dozen words for me. And my best friend in Connecticut taught me a few German phrases.

Ms. Taylor wrote numerous notes and asked how I would handle an assortment of delicate, in-flight situations.

I answered to the best of my ability, but basically I just winged it. I felt my pleasant and helpful attitude was what she was really wanted to hear.

Miss Taylor also inquired about any legal issues I might have. "Can you pass a military clearance?"

She next requested, "Please stand, walk to the office door, turn slowly around, stop, and walk back to me."

She scrutinized me as I did what she requested. I stood as tall and straight as possible, and she wrote additional comments on my application.

"Can you be ready next week?" Miss Taylor asked. "You'll have to pass a physical with the company doctor. On Monday, we begin classes."

"Yes, I'll definitely be ready."

"I'll call the doctor and set up an appointment for tomorrow morning at ten," she replied.

What a surprise to be approved so quickly.

My acceptance, however, applied only to the training period. I still had to pass the final exams. I'd be competing with other topnotch attendees for a limited number of positions.

"The competition will be intense," Miss Taylor explained. "So be prepared."

When I returned to my apartment, Barbara and Carole rushed me as I entered.

"How did it go?"

"I made the first cut. I still have to pass a physical and the school exams," I explained. "I'll know in four weeks if I actually make it."

While we continued to chat, I learned that their expected roommate would not be arriving after all. Consequently, I remained renting with them for a total of three years, all because of our chance encounter at the YWCA.

That evening I called my parents. Standing in the living room by the glass doors overlooking the lights of San Francisco, I told them of my school acceptance.

"How exciting," my mother exclaimed. "Tell me, what was the interview like? When do your classes begin? When do you graduate?"

My father, however, angrily opposed my change of careers.

"This is not why I paid your college bills," he asserted. "I think you've made a poor decision."

Being over twenty-one and three thousand miles away, he could only protest. I disliked going against his will; my father was the rock in our family. But I realized I had to stand up for my own preferences.

AIRLINE SCHOOL

"Good morning, ladies. Please be seated."

Ms. Taylor stood in the front of the classroom and greeted the prospective flight attendants. Her dark hair fell to her pink blouse, and she wore a striped scarf around her neck. Next, she handed out thick training manuals.

"Look these over," she instructed. "I'll highlight the areas you'll need to know by heart."

We sat four abreast at six-foot-long tables, dressed in our best office attire. Eight tables shared the large instruction room. I knew no one and introduced myself to the gal sitting to my right.

"Hi. I'm Bobbi. Are you from California?"

"Sarah. Thank you. I'm from Switzerland," she answered with a slight accent.

What a gorgeous woman. Sarah had platinum blond hair cut in a short bob and a flawless complexion. She wore a navy skirt with a white blouse and gold pin. She was one of the most beautiful women I had ever seen. I immediately felt awed, but she smiled and said, "I'm so glad you said hello. I don't know anyone."

"Neither do I. If you need help, let me know and we can study together."

Just then, a short, balding man entered the room. He sat on the corner of a front table, looking us over and smiling. Once he noticed Sarah, he couldn't keep his eyes off her. Her beauty was that striking.

"Please welcome Mr. Daly, the owner of World Airways," Miss Taylor said. His stocky build and jovial nature belied his aggressive character.

"In 1950," Miss Taylor continued, "when Mr. Daly was only twenty-seven, he bought the organization. Since then, he has expanded it into one of the largest nonscheduled airlines in the world."

Mr. Daly stood as we applauded him.

"Thank you. And thank you for applying," he said. "I look forward to having you join my company."

After Mr. Daly left, Ms. Taylor said, "Please call me Diane." She then pointed to a dark-haired young woman sitting in the front row by the window.

"Tell me your name," Ms. Taylor requested. "And where are you from?"

An Asian woman started the introduction process. Thick, black hair framed her attractive face, and her dark eyes sparkled when she said, "My name is Emily Chin. I'm originally from Hong Kong. I now live in San Francisco."

More introductions were made. Half the students were residents of foreign countries, mostly from Europe. They sported all shades of skin and hair color.

At the end of the day, as we were scooting back our chairs and getting up to leave, Diane cautioned us, "Be ready for a rough four weeks. Only fifteen of you will be asked to join the airline."

We glanced around the room. There were roughly thirty women in the class. Was it true? Half of us would be gone by the end of the month? Who would remain? Would I?

Before we left, Diane took measurements for our uniforms.

"They are specifically designed for international travel by the Joseph Magnin Company," she said.

I didn't know the company but learned that it was a high-end fashion store in San Francisco. The camel-colored uniform consisted of a skirt, a jacket, two shells (white cotton for summer and camel wool for winter), and a jockey-style hat.

"Upon graduation," Diane continued, "you'll also receive a coat, a purse, an in-flight apron, and a suitcase. You'll need to buy plain pumps, high heels, boots and leather gloves—all in black, along with white cotton gloves. However, don't buy them until after graduation."

Although World paid us to attend school, we were not officially hired. Once we passed the final exams and completed the physical, we then became legitimate flight attendants.

During the next three days we attended the Patricia Stevens Modeling School and learned the finer points of grooming. "You are not to wear any jewelry except for a modest watch and ring," the instructor said. "No necklaces or earrings."

Sarah sat in a salon chair and I took a seat next to her. A beautician trimmed her hair and another cut mine to shoulder length. "If you grow it longer, you'll need to wrap it in a bun or a French twist."

Back at the modeling schoolroom, we learned to check in and out of hotels, to proceed through international customs, and to look professional at all times.

"World Airways requires their airline crews to hire porters," the modeling instructor said. "They don't want you lugging your suitcases through airports." Suitcases with rollers had not been invented and our silver luggage was heavy.

With our backs as straight as yardsticks, she taught us to walk in unison like attractive robots.

After modeling school, we returned to World's office building and inspected a mock-up galley with ovens and coffeemakers. We were handed the following card:

FIRST-CLASS SERVICE SCHEDULE

Before take-off:

1. Pass hard candy, magazines, pillows, and blankets.

2. Pass five-cigarette packages with matchbooks bearing our airline logo.

Once the plane reaches cruising altitude:

3. Pass hot scented towels

4. Clean up.

5. Pass hors d'oeuvres.

6. Clean up.

7. Pass two mini-bottles of hard liquor. A glass with ice. Sodas and water.

8. Clean up.

9. Pass dinner trays containing the entrée, salad, dessert, roll, and split of wine.

10. Pass coffee, tea, milk, and champagne.

11. Clean up.

12. Pass two mini-bottles of after-dinner drinks.

13. Clean up.

"Conducting all these services in a plane loaded with passengers will mean you'll be on your feet for hours," Diane said. "Work quickly and keep smiling."

Diane continued with her instructions and showed us how to set up the galley for a full meal service and how to make coffee.

"The ovens will come packed with entrees from the catering company. Confirm with them that you've received the required amount of trays for all the scheduled services.

"After each meal, make sure you lock the cabinets and secure the galley counter," Diane cautioned. "In rough weather, these can become dangerous missiles."

Although her instructions were helpful, they were relatively basic and superficial. It wasn't until we actually worked the galley during flight that we gained speed and accuracy. The real test came when doing the job on a shaking plane with a hundred impatient passengers waiting to be served.

The following day we practiced and memorized the public address or PA announcements. We stood in front of our classmates with a mock airplane telephone at our lips and recited the departing and landing speeches. Before long we knew the words by heart and no longer had to read the printed forms. Foreign and U.S. customs papers were explained to us in detail, and we were tested on both the documents and inflight announcements the next day.

During the last three weeks we learned evacuation procedures, health guidelines, and airplane construction. The daily exams became much harder.

As students, we operated window and door exits and jumped into emergency chutes, long orange troughs that unfurled from the exit doors to the tarmac below. Diane showed us how to use fire extinguishers, to administer oxygen, and to perform CPR.

We were required to understand all emergency methods backwards and forwards. Knowing them on paper and knowing them on the airplane involved numerous pre-boarding tests and hard experience. The more we worked as flight attendants, the more we learned to respond with complete accuracy.

One day my classmates and I executed a ditch simulation in San Francisco Bay. A huge, yellow raft bobbed about on the surface with twenty students aboard, clad in bathing suits. Greta and Rike, two German recruits, joined Sarah and me at one end of the raft. We laughed as we splashed in the Bay, yet mentally took notes of all required actions for the upcoming tests. And we carried knives. In case of a ditching, we were to use them to cut the lanyard separating the raft from the airplane.

Our classes also involved "arm and cross check" drills.

"Flight attendants must attach the metal bar located under the exit door's container to the floor hooks," Diane said. "In an emergency landing, the slide will automatically deploy if the door is opened." She added, "You need to disarm the chute once the plane lands so the gate agent is not struck by the deploying slide."

Evacuation procedures are very important in the airline industry. The Federal Aviation Administration, or FAA, requires all planes to be emptied in ninety seconds, no matter the size.

"Even in our Boeing jets with 186 passengers, we must get everyone out in ninety seconds," Diane said.

Each year, all airlines must do a simulated evacuation. It occurs in a pitch-black hanger with friends and relatives acting as passengers. During the process, half the exits are blocked to imitate possible fire or water obstructions. The flight attendants do not know in advance which exits will be blocked, and they have to adjust their passenger instructions and movements accordingly.

Besides taking exams and studying, we had to have inoculations every other day. Shots for smallpox, cholera, tetanus, yellow fever, and typhoid were required for international travel.

We also visited numerous consulates in San Francisco. For every country where our airline had a layover, we were to obtain a visa.

The month of training created a sister-like bond among those who remained. Greta, Rike, Sarah, and I lunched together and studied the manual. I learned that Rike was an artist, Greta loved cooking, and Sarah's father was a diplomat.

"Our classmates are disappearing," Greta remarked. No one informed us why the number of students declined, but each morning we noticed more empty chairs.

One day, Sarah was gone. I was surprised and saddened by her departure and didn't know how to contact her. She was part of our foursome. But Diane was right. Only fifteen would graduate that month.

A small ceremony was conducted on the fourth Friday of our month-long training. We gathered in the classroom, laughing and congratulating each other, so proud that we had completed the challenging course of instruction. Family and friends took seats in the back of the room with some standing against the wall. Diane pinned wings to our new, form-fitting uniforms, and everyone clapped in appreciation.

"With this class, we now have a total of eighty flight attendants working for World Airways," she announced. "The following specialties are what each new graduate brings to our airline."

How surprised I was to hear her say, "Please welcome Bobbi Phelps, a college graduate from Connecticut who speaks five languages."

My face turned bright red as I rose to accept my wings. With all the composure I could muster, I smiled at the audience and unashamedly basked in their applause.

My parents telephoned that Sunday evening and I told them about my graduation. Mom was thrilled and shared words of encouragement. Dad listened to my excitement but remained silent.

FIRST CLASS TO ITALY

"Yes! We got it!" I raised my arms in triumph as we stood in the dispatch office in Oakland. "We're flying to Rome!"

Cindy, Gail, and I had our flight bids accepted. We would be together for the next month, flying most of the time between the East Coast and Europe. Our first trip had us working a flight from California to Italy. Our passengers were a group of wealthy opera aficionados.

Whenever our airline was chartered by a group of affluent tourists, they received outstanding service. Charter planes were not divided between first, business, and tourist classes; the passengers enjoyed one category of service, whatever type the group had contracted. The opera organization requested first-class benefits.

We had been on duty two hours before the California passengers boarded at the Oakland terminal. Standing at the bottom of the aft ramp, I smiled and said, "Welcome aboard." I could feel their enthusiasm as they walked up the portable stairs.

As the cabin crew helped them find their seats, I passed out blankets, pillows, and hard candy. Dissolving the candies provided relief to those with ear-pressure issues. We also distributed cigarettes, matchbooks, slippers, and eyeshades.

As the travelers were settling in, we demonstrated the use of life vests and oxygen masks. Finally, I returned to the rear jump seat and prepared for take-off. Before landing ten hours later, we would endure a marathon of services: dinner and breakfast meals, hors d'oeuvres, and four beverage dispersals.

We left Oakland right on time, and after donning our leather-like aprons we passed out hot towels scented with lemon. From the back, Cindy and I began a liquor distribution while Gail set up the galley for dinner.

"You'll receive two mini-bottles," I told the passengers. "Do you want rum, whisky, vodka, bourbon, scotch, or gin?"

Standing by their seats, Cindy and I added soda, water, and ice as they requested. They couldn't believe they were getting two bottles each.

The next course was hot hors d'oeuvres. Colorful shish kabobs, lying in steaming juices, lined a deep, silver tray.

Walking backwards, Cindy picked a skewer from the tray I held. She used tongs to rest it on a doily-covered plate and presented the kabob to a passenger. We worked as a well-coordinated team among a happy group of well-sloshed travelers.

They called to each other and chatted around us, oblivious to our movements. As I walked up the aisle, a man on my left abruptly rose from his seat.

His shoulder collided with my tray and flipped it in the air. It landed upside down on a woman on the opposite side of the aisle.

"NO! NO! NO!" she screamed, rising to her feet. "I can't believe it! This whole plane and you had to dump it on me!"

Globs of dark sauce and chunks of meat and vegetables smothered her beautiful white suit. She was plastered from the tip of her collar to the hem of her skirt.

I apologized profusely and attempted to wipe off the worst of the mess, but she continued berating me.

"It had to happen to me! You! You've ruined my whole vacation!"

I was practically in tears from her fierce tirade.

"Please come with me," I said. "Let's get you changed. We'll use a restroom at the back of the plane."

As she followed me down the aisle, she showed the other passengers how terrible she looked. As if they couldn't see for themselves.

"Gail, do you have some extra clothes?"

With one look at the once-white suit, Gail started to giggle. She quickly placed a hand over her mouth and covered her smile.

"Hi, I'm Gail. I have a blouse and slacks that will definitely fit you."

The woman grudgingly stuck out her hand. "I'm Mrs. Manning. Anything is better than this."

I helped Mrs. Manning replace her damaged suit with Gail's extra clothes. She was feeling slightly better when I loaned her an apron and pinned on my wings. It might have been the liquor, but from then on she loved every minute of the flight. She helped clean trays, visited with the passengers, and thoroughly enjoyed being a flight attendant.

As the cabin crew passed out after-dinner drinks (again, two mini-bottles each), I poured champagne. Popping champagne bottles can be quite dangerous. During airline school I learned to slowly twist the bottle and gradually ease out the cork. On first-class voyages, opening champagne bottles became my specialty.

After the shish kabob spill, I washed Mrs. Manning's suit in the lavatory and hung it in our coat rack. By the time we approached Rome the suit was dry and had resumed its original shape and color.

As the plane began to descend, a child started to scream. With the altitude change, air pressure in the cabin increased. The five-year-old boy was responding to his ears being blocked. I grabbed some hard candy and gave them to his mother.

"Have him suck on one of these," I told her. "Get him to yawn. That'll also help."

I left them to wake Mrs. Manning. I needed to return her clothes and retrieve my apron and wings. While she was changing, Cindy, Gail, and I walked through the cabin. We checked to make sure all tray tables and window shades were up and that the passengers had their seat belts fastened. We then handed coats and hats to the still inebriated passengers.

Once Mrs. Manning had dressed in her white suit, I handed her a cleaner's coupon.

"Please forgive me," I said. "I am so sorry for the mess and inconvenience you endured."

Mrs. Manning thanked me for taking such good care of her and handed me back the coupon.

"I should apologize to you," she replied. "I didn't mean to yell."

As she left the plane, I noticed how stunning she looked in her sparkling white suit, not a spot of grease anywhere. With one last glance, she threw me a kiss and entered the Rome terminal.

NEW YORK CITY GLAMOUR

"Look at them," a teenager exclaimed to his father, pointing at us while we marched through the New York airport.

"Aren't they pretty?" the elder man replied.

Men smiled and women looked at us with envy. The five of us were all slim and groomed, with the same make-up, hairdos, and stylish uniforms. We walked in unison, side by side, carrying black purses draped over our shoulders.

We had just returned from Paris. Our airline crew had four days to layover in New York City before flying back to Europe. The station manager had booked us into the Statler Hilton.

We arrived at the hotel's entrance in a black stretch limousine, listening to honking horns and screeching brakes through the open windows. A porter held the car door open, and one uniformed crew member after another stepped out. A valet took our luggage and nearby side-walk strollers stopped to stare. If our uniforms had been black and white, we would have looked like a parade of penguins.

Yes, during the sixties and seventies the airline industry was the place to be. What other occupation paid for its employees to stay at topnotch hotels in exotic locations, allowed them to shop at the best stores worldwide, and gave them exceptional wages? I made three times what I had earned as a legal secretary, and I worked half the days. Granted, the workdays were exceptionally long, but they were always exciting.

Once when we ferried a plane to a new location, Captain Chapman asked, "Hey, Bobbi. Want to watch the landing?"

"Sure, I'd love to."

For the first time, a captain allowed me to sit on the small jump seat in the cockpit. It was humbling to listen to the crew go through their checklists. I had often heard the professional chatter between the control tower and the flight deck whenever I delivered meals. But to hear it as our plane approached the airstrip was awesome. I watched the runway come up to meet the wheels, heard the tires screech, and saw the landing strip lights rush by at lightning speed.

As an international flight attendant, I traveled throughout the Orient and most of Europe. Because our destinations could change, we always packed bathing suits and boots. We could fly one day to sunny Hawaii and a few days later to snowy Alaska. From check-in at dispatch to check-in at a hotel, my flight duties could last up to thirty hours. But when we arrived, we had two to ten days off...a lot of time to explore foreign cultures and unusual customs.

Many of my fellow flight attendants joined me on my explorations. We were considered ambassadors for the airline company, not only on the plane but when we traveled on our own. We had to be impeccable and act with absolute grace—always.

Penn Station and Madison Square Garden were located across the street from the Statler Hilton. The hotel's number was easy to remember: Pennsylvania 6-5000, made famous in the early forties by Glenn Miller and his band.

New York City was an explorer's paradise. We went to rodeos, concerts, and dog shows at the Garden. We watched the skaters at Rockefeller Center in the winter, took carriage rides in Central Park in spring, and visited the Guggenheim Museum in summer.

There was always danger, however, when staying in a large city. In 1966, two United Airlines flight attendants were attacked at their Seattle hotel. They had left their room door ajar for their third roommate, still out on a date. By the time she returned, one of the flight attendants had been killed and the other bludgeoned. This type of news traveled quickly through the airline industry. From then on, whenever I checked into a hotel room, I had the bellhop wait while I searched under the bed, in the closet, and in the bathroom.

Whenever my crew had a long layover in New York, I invited my roommates to join me in Connecticut. My parents lived an hour by train from Grand Central Station and they happily welcomed my flying friends. A few months earlier Greta and Rike joined me on one long layover in New York, and I was pleased to show them an American home in the woods of Connecticut.

Surprisingly, my father, who initially hated my profession, now became a delightful host. He had succumbed to the beauty and charm of the flight attendants, and I became a source of pride to my parents.

While in New York, I overheard a business friend ask my father, "What does Bobbi do?"

"Why, she's an international flight attendant," he answered, standing a little taller. "With her airline discounts, Florence and I flew to Hawaii last year. We've been to England, Spain, Morocco…."

His voice trailed off as he listed country after country. I felt thrilled that he had finally accepted my occupation. I had been rewarded for my determination and hard work.

Back at the Statler Hilton, I stood in my uniform behind the co-pilot at the front desk. My mind had wandered. I had been thinking about my parents and the glamour we enjoyed as flight attendants. Suddenly, Connie poked me.

"You're next," she said.

"May I help you?" the receptionist asked.

Just then we heard a rowdy noise coming from the mezzanine. We all looked up, and I recognized a very drunk Marlene wobbling close to the iron railing. She swore loudly and hurled brash comments at the decorative plants lining the balustrade.

Marlene, a beautiful, robust blond, was a member of a different crew of flight attendants staying in New York. Known for being a fun-loving German, Marlene was both entertaining and diligent. You always had a good time with her, but you never knew what to expect.

"Go get her," the hotel manager yelled at a baggage handler.

He raced up the stairs just as Marlene, her back to the lobby, pulled down her underpants and squatted. From my viewpoint at the reception desk, I could see a yellow stream falling from between her legs to the mezzanine floor.

"Oh no!" I gasped.

The bellhop rushed Marlene and tried to help her stand. In her drunken stupor she thought she was in her hotel bathroom and a strange man had just entered. She quickly pulled up her pants and gave the employee a strong shove backwards. Another bellhop engaged Marlene and the two men struggled to control her. Grasping her arms, they escorted her to the elevator and back to her room.

I glanced at the manager and hoped he had not recognized Marlene as one of our employees. Lowering my head, I continued to fill out the hotel's paperwork.

"So much for glamour," I thought.

After unpacking and showering in my room, I experienced a restless night of sleep when the telephone rang. Groggy and half asleep, I heard Connie on the other end.

"Join us downstairs," she said. "We're going exploring."

"Go on without me," I said, yawning into the phone. "I'll meet up later."

Large, prickly rollers in my hair had kept me from a decent night of sleep. I fell back into bed for a couple more hours. Since I grew up near the city, I preferred to rest. I met them the next day in the hotel lobby.

"Let's take a cab," I said. "Otherwise, it's quite a hike."

They readily agreed. We took a yellow taxi to Radio City Music Hall and watched Love Story with Ali

MacGraw and Ryan O'Neal. The legendary Rockettes performed afterwards.

"The matinee movie and show cost only $1.25." I remarked. "Where can you get a deal like that?"

"Can you believe how high they kicked?" Connie commented. "And in complete harmony."

"I counted thirty-six girls," observed Robin. "We'd be hard pressed to do that with just the three of us."

After the show we had an early dinner at the Russian Tea Room, a dimly lit restaurant with green walls and red banquettes. The smell of coffee and cigarettes hit us the moment we pushed through the revolving doors. We ordered Polish dinners and a glass of vodka each.

From there we walked to the Top of the Sixes, a restaurant and bar at 666 Fifth Avenue. Dressed in miniskirts, we sat at a window table overlooking the city. While we discussed the movie, complimentary champagne flutes arrived with a note from a male customer.

"Please be my guest," it said.

We turned around and saw an older gentleman in the corner. With a smile and a nod of his head, he raised his glass and saluted us.

"Now, that's what I like about being a flight attendant," I said.

"What a life," Robin countered.

We sat drinking our champagne and looking at the lights of the city. We really did have a remarkable life.

MAINE MISHAP

A tourist group from Northern California chartered our airline for a flight to Europe. Their trip originated in Oakland and terminated in Gatwick, England, thirty miles south of London. We had a refueling stop in Maine before the jet headed across the Atlantic.

Nonstop liquor flowed, and the passengers became highly vocal and energized. They laughed, sang, and called out to each other, moving from seat to seat and joking with friends.

They settled down as we approached Bangor. Being from New England, I loved our Maine layovers. It gave me plenty of time to enjoy lobster dinners and shop for antiques. This time we landed for refueling only.

The passengers returned to their seats, strapped themselves in, and prepared for landing. I sat in my assigned seat, on the aisle in the rear section of the plane.

Just as we touched down I heard an explosion. The right-hand, aft window exit had opened. A bright orange banner streamed from the wing.

The jet raced down the runway as all flight attendants stayed fastened in their seats. Bells went off in the
cockpit. As soon as the jet slowed, engineer Bill Stringer
emerged. He wore a concerned expression on his face. The
opening of the aft window exit compromised and activated
the chute in the wing, simulating an evacuation.

Bill and I approached the nearby passengers and
asked, "What happened?"

"I was hot, so I opened the window," answered a
man in a high state of inebriation. In his defiant stupor,
he seemed to think his action was appropriate and even
funny.

"After the passengers get off, the captain will need
to talk with you," Bill said. "What's your name?"

"John Smith," he smirked and turned his back on
Bill. I thought the engineer was going to grab his jacket
and yank him out of his seat. But he kept his cool and
walked back to the cockpit.

No one can open an emergency exit when a plane
is in the air. The aircraft pressure makes it impossible. But
once the jet lands, the pressure is released. That's when
"John Smith" snapped the lever to the open position.

Mr. Smith deplaned with the other passengers and
mingled in the crowd, trying to hide. While we waited to
hear the prognosis of our flight, local officials escorted him
to a side office. The captain and engineer confronted him
while police officers took notes.

We spent five hours in the Bangor terminal waiting
for a replacement evacuation chute to be sent from Wash-
ington, D.C. Besides wasting time and inconveniencing
passengers, it cost our airline thousands of dollars to replace
and install the new slide.

As the hours passed, people in the tour group grumbled. Many had missed connecting flights. The Bangor terminal was small and had only a few chairs. The tourists began to slide to the floor, sitting with their backs against the cold wall.

Finally we were instructed to reboard. We walked to our assigned stations and watched the passengers board the jet like sleepy sheep. They returned to their original seats and fell fast asleep.

On the flight to England I asked Evelyn, the senior flight attendant, what would happen to Mr. Smith.

"Mr. Smith is an attorney. If our airline sues him, he said he'd sue us right back."

"What could he sue for?" I questioned.

"Supposedly he didn't know that it wasn't a window," she said.

Mr. Smith informed the local police that our plane did not have an appropriate sign. We needed a notice stating that the exit should only be opened in an emergency. Today, planes have signs that say just that. Because our plane did not, there were no repercussions for Mr. Smith.

ENGLISH GHOSTS

The next week we worked a flight from New York to England. Most of the time we flew into Gatwick, but this time we were scheduled to land at Heathrow, unloading tourists for the Wimbledon Tennis finals. All London hotels were booked. Consequently, we took traditional taxis, black boxes with vertical grills, to Surrey, about an hour away.

Our airline booked us at the Selsdon Park Hotel in Sanderstead, a huge Victorian manor house that had been converted to a four-star resort. We drove up a long drive-way and parked before an ivy-covered brick mansion with multi-paned windows outlined in white. The hotel was situated on two hundred acres. We were going to hike, walk through elaborate gardens, and play croquet.

Once we checked in, I noticed an elderly lady wearing black clothes and a veil. She had entered the reception area after the other crew members had gone to their rooms. The thin dowager held two tiny dogs on leashes and let them lift their legs on an antique table in the lobby. Pale liquid dripped down the spindles and onto the oriental carpet.

When the woman left, I asked, "Who was that? Why didn't you ask her to control her dogs?"

Selsdon Park Hotel, Surrey, England.

"We don't ask her to do anything," the clerk answered. "She lives in the hotel and her family has financial interests here."

"So that's why there are so many fancy cars in the parking lot," I said.

There were at least three Rolls Royce limousines parked at the far side of the front entrance. I shook my head in disgust and walked to my room.

The crew had been assigned to an older section of the hotel. My room was on the ground floor with French doors opening to a garden setting. The small room connected to Susanne's room via the bathroom. We had goose down comforters, and when we went to sleep at night, hot water bottles were placed in our beds.

During the day, Susanne, Judy, and I walked the grounds and challenged a few guests to a game of croquet: flight attendants versus tourists. We put up a rousing battle but the tourists won, and they invited us for tea that afternoon.

At night all five flight attendants gathered in a small alcove to tell stories. We sat on a sofa under a niche of the rising staircase and shared a bottle of wine. Our section of the large manor house had been built in the 1500s. In the darkness we sipped red wine, watched a lantern glow on the coffee table, and told ghost stories.

Two staff members joined our conversation. They informed us that the hotel was indeed haunted. The drafty hallways created scary noises, and they told tales of unusual encounters.

"We often hear strange sounds. And I saw a shadowy figure moving along a supposedly vacant hallway just last week."

They filled our minds with spooks, and we huddled closer in the dark alcove. A pale, orange light filtered through the nook and the smell of lantern oil coated the air. The employees continued with their ghost stories.

After a few drinks we blew out the lamp and separated. Judy, Susanne, and I walked down a gloomy corridor to our rooms, whispering about the employees' comments.

That night Susanne and I called to each other through the connecting bathroom, making sure we were each secure in our bedrooms. Judy, located further down the hall, did not have a roommate.

She locked the hall door after entering her room, but forgot to check the French doors that opened to the garden. During the night she heard them creak open. She sat straight up in bed and screamed.

"Who's there?" she yelled.

The flight engineer's room was next door to Judy's suite and he banged on her door.

"Are you all right?" he asked.

"I am now. But I was scared to death. I forgot to lock the French doors, and one blew open."

They both went back to their own rooms, but Judy couldn't sleep. She kept seeing moon shadows from the trees bouncing across her walls. Shivering in bed, Judy slept for only a couple of hours. She vowed to never again listen to ghost stories while staying in a haunted hotel.

IRISH FLIGHTS

On many of our flights to Europe, our airline flew by way of Shannon, Ireland. Our layovers were usually just a couple of days, but occasionally we were given extra time. On this particular layover, Sally, Kris, and I rented a taxi and traveled a few hours to the Waterford crystal factory.

Stopping at a pub along the way, we learned that since we didn't have a man to escort us, we had to enter a side door and sit in a separate area from the male patrons. We had fish and chips and a couple of mugs of beer.

The three of us clicked our glasses and broke into song. "Leaving on a Jet Plane" was our favorite. The men on the other side of the pub came to our side and joined in the singing. We easily could have wasted our time away, but we had major shopping to do. Soon after, we left for the historic city of Waterford.

At the factory we bought crystal by the box load. Lamps, bowls, glasses, and vases packed the taxi's floor and trunk (or *boot*, as the English say). The beer eased our wallets and helped with the purchases. Soon the vehicle had no room to spare.

Later, on our departure back to New York, we entered the duty-free section of the Irish airport. Continuing with our shopping spree, we bought wool blankets, liquor, linen, and handmade sweaters.

In 1966, U. S. customs taxed everything over one hundred dollars. Consequently, we arranged to have our purchases divided into increments. Every time we departed Shannon, we took another box home to America.

During our Irish layovers we often toured castles and historic homes in nearby areas. The green farmland was dotted with sheep and ancient buildings were scattered throughout the countryside.

The Bunratty Castle, built in the 1400s, was situated close to the airport and our hotel. Kris, Sally, and I chose to attend one of their medieval banquets on the last night of our layover. We walked through the kitchen garden and stopped to smell the fragrant herbs within its high walls. After exploring a number of castle rooms, we joined the other tourists and sat in the large dining room.

Medieval tapestries hung throughout the Grand Hall and antique furniture with life-sized woodcarvings graced the stone floor. Local entertainers dressed in period costumes danced and sang to our clapping appreciation. One played the harp and another the violin.

At one end of the hall, I noticed the skeleton head of a huge deer attached to the top of the wall. The tour guide told us the deer, which had once been common in Ireland, had been extinct for thousands of years. Its antlers spread across nine feet. Bog hunters discovered the carcass in a neighboring marsh in the 18th century.

We joined the other tourists at long tables and ate

bread and deer meat. A knife was our only utensil. Sally, Kris, and I chomped on meat and broke loaves of bread to dip into sauces. Throughout the meal we gulped large mugs of mead, a wine made from fermented honey.

With no napkins and gravy coating our hands and dripping down our chins, we certainly seemed like the medieval maidens of yesteryear. No longer were we the glamorous flight attendants of a few days ago.

Soon it was time to leave. A traditional black taxi returned us to our hotel. The narrow road, lined on both sides with stonewalls, went directly toward Shannon. In the distance we saw our hotel lights shimmering in the fog.

The following day we flew Gaelic passengers to Boston. They wore their very best clothes, wool suits in tweed patterns with matching hats for both the men and women.

Surprisingly, they barely spoke English. Our airline hired a Gaelic flight attendant to translate the announcements. In spite of knowing French and Spanish, I couldn't understand a word the interpreter said.

Because of the language barrier, the passengers chatted among themselves. On our arrival in Massachusetts, they beamed with happy expectations as they descended the portable stairs.

OKTOBERFEST IN MUNICH

"Look at this room," I said to Rike. "I love the white linens and lace curtains."

"It looks so clean and bright," Rike responded. "They even gave us fresh daisies."

We embraced the quaint room of the local German inn. Although the walls were dark wood, the twin beds sported puffy white goose-down pillows, mattresses, and coverlets. The large window looked into a village square surrounded by three-story buildings, with a spouting fountain in the center.

Exhausted from working a long flight across the Atlantic, we showered and folded into our beds like clams in soft white shells. A slight breeze blew through the curtains. The room was chilly but we were pleasantly warm, nestled beneath our down-filled comforters. While lying in our beds, I rolled to face Rike.

"My parents love to hear my airline stories," I said. "I can't wait to tell them about Oktoberfest."

"I don't have much of a family," Rike answered.

"My parents and I escaped East Germany by going through the iron curtain. My father didn't make it."

Her comment saddened me. Rike added more details of her journey from East Berlin, and despite her dramatic teenage years she had a smile that radiated whenever she spoke.

In the hotel lobby the next morning, we met Greta, the other German in our crew, and Kathy, a Canadian from Halifax. We all had breakfast and waited for Heidi. She was a cute Austrian with iridescent red hair.

She told us, "I'll join you as soon as I finish ironing."

The five of us bonded during our many European flights. I was the only American in our crew. Greta, the senior flight attendant, had a thick, blond braid that hung from the left side of her head down to her waist. Her parents lived in Stuttgart. She had traveled to South America the previous year. It was from listening to her stories that I decided to venture around the world, and did so after I stopped flying a few years later.

Kathy, tall with black hair and blue eyes, was once an advertising model. Heidi was short in stature and the most organized of the bunch. Each one of us brought something different to our friendship.

With our European friends, Kathy and I explored Germany with ease. We shopped for Rosenthal crystal, rode horses in nearby forests, and ate at little-known Bavarian restaurants. One time we dressed up and rented a private box at the famous opera house in Stuttgart. Rike, Greta, and Heidi revealed a country we never could have discovered if we had been by ourselves as typical tourists.

During one of our Atlantic crossings, Heidi introduced Kathy and me to *Stern*, a German magazine similar in size to our *Look* and *Life* Magazines. Taking a break from passing and cleaning food trays, Kathy and I glanced at the magazine as we sat on a rear jump seat. We stared at photographs of nude people and depictions of intercourse, masturbation, and prostitution. While growing up, both Kathy and I had been sheltered sexually. *Stern* was a revelation for us, the naïve North Americans.

While critiquing European magazines and morals, Rike told us about a dinner date her Swedish roommate, Anna, had at a small restaurant in Berkeley. Anna (also a flight attendant) met her lover Seth at the café, and sat at a table for two near the back of the room. As it had been drizzling, they both wore raincoats. Drinking wine and enjoying their loving relationship, they held hands across the table and waited for dinner to arrive.

Anna reached under the table and brought Seth's foot up to her lap. She removed his sandal and massaged his toes. While they were both immersed in their conversation and wine, she slipped his bare foot under her coat and into her crotch. She had nothing on.

Seth practically jumped from the table. Then he settled back down, placing his foot again between her legs.

The European flight attendants definitely had a different perspective on love and relationships. Surprisingly, I never knew of any sexual activities developing between the European cabin crew and our passengers or cockpit men.

At the end of September, the five of us worked a special flight to Munich. Our airline transported a group of insurance employees to Oktoberfest, a sixteen-day holiday in Germany. Its main purpose is to promote and celebrate beer.

After resting overnight, we ventured outside to a nearby tent-covered field. We sat on benches at long tables, surrounded by young men and women who were drinking and singing.

The blond, buxom waitresses wore the national costume of Germany, the dirndl—a tight, low-cut bodice over a white, short-sleeved blouse, with a full skirt and apron. They carried three or four heavy mugs in each hand, filled with beer. The dimpled glass mugs held thirty-four ounces of beer apiece, and their arm muscles bulged from the weight.

The waiters wore grey lederhosen, or leather shorts, with high socks, suspenders, and fitted jackets. They passed huge pretzels, as well as sausage and sauerkraut dishes, to those at the tables. The smell of the food only enhanced our desire for more beer.

Oktoberfest beer contains more alcohol than regular German beer. And after a mug each, we added our voices to the crowd.

For hours we sang rousing songs, ate pretzels, and drank with the locals. Under the gigantic canvas tent, the five of us became silly and sentimental. We held tightly to each other and continued to sing.

"Ein mass, bitte," I shouted. *One more, please,* as I ordered second mugs of beer for all five of us.

The smells of German food wafted through the air and whetted our appetite. Enthusiastically, we tried to order more beer.

"Time to go home," Heidi announced. She had cut us off.

We wrapped our arms around each other's waists and swayed from one side of the path to the other as we sauntered back to our hotel.

As international flight attendants, most of our activities involved cheerful times, where we enhanced our friendships and explored different countries. On one flight, however, our fun-loving attitudes changed to strict professionalism.

TRAGEDY IN THE AIR

Transporting military families to and from Germany was routine for my airline. Many of our flights ended at the Rhein-Main Air Base in Frankfurt. The base was closed in 2005, but at the time we were flying it was the most active military terminal in Europe. On one of our flights back to the United States, army families crowded the plane with children, baby bags, and colorful toys.

After serving beverages and meals, I joined Greta on the front jump seat. Although she was the senior flight attendant and essentially my boss, we were good friends and often skied and visited together during our days off.

About two-thirds of the way across the Atlantic the call button chimed, illuminating the panel above a seat in the back of the cabin. Rike, Kathy, and Heidi, the three rear flight attendants, were alerted. A passenger needed assistance. In the forward galley I entertained a couple of children with card tricks while the aft crew handled the call.

"Is there a doctor on board?" Rike asked over the

PA system.

No one came forward. With a plane full of military passengers, it was unusual not to have a doctor, nurse, or medic on board. Without a medical person, the flight attendants took over.

"Watch the cockpit and galley," Greta said as she walked toward the rear of the plane.

She found a father supporting his two-year old son while the mother stood close by. The frantic parents said they couldn't wake their son. He had cold hands and feet, yet he was hot with fever. Standing in the dimly lit galley with Rike holding a flashlight, Kathy checked the boy's mouth for any obstructions. The boy was not breathing.

Heidi placed a blanket on the floor near the aft door, and Kathy gently rested the toddler on top. She tilted his head back, lifted his chin, and closed his nostrils. While Kathy knelt and started mouth-to-mouth resuscitation, Rike pushed down on his chest. Crammed into the small space by the rear exit, the two counted.

"One, two, three, four, five, six, seven, breathe. One, two, three, four, five, six, seven, breathe."

Greta notified Captain Rogers. He planned to dump fuel and make an emergency landing as soon as the plane reached the mainland, more than an hour away.

In the meantime, Kathy and Rike kept performing CPR and Heidi relieved them whenever one became overly tired. Greta suspended the beverage service and asked the parents, Mr. and Mrs. Southwick, about the child and his health.

"Brian has been sick for the past two weeks," Mr. Southwick said. "We took him to an ER a few days ago. The doctor suggested we wait before traveling home."

Since it was only a suggestion and Brian seemed to be better, they decided to go ahead with the flight.

Captain Rogers arrived at the rear galley and listened to the parents' concerns. He told them about his arrangements with the local hospital.

"We'll be making an emergency landing just as soon as we reach the airfield," he said. "Your son will be transported by ambulance to the nearest hospital."

The three flight attendants steadily performed CPR on Brian. Five minutes had passed since the father had first carried him to the rear. Kathy, Heidi, and Rike continued with the process for another thirty minutes.

Soon, they were exhausted. Their knees and backs ached. They paused and rocked back on their heels.

"Please don't stop," the mother wailed.

"I'm so sorry," Kathy sympathized. "He hasn't moved or responded since we started. He still is not breathing."

"I'll tell the captain," said Heidi and walked toward the cockpit.

Kathy wrapped the boy in a blanket. Rike moved passengers from the last row and let Mrs. Southwick sit by the window, hugging the covered child to her chest. Her husband seated himself next to her, and they cried and held each other for the remainder of the flight.

As soon as we landed and taxied to the terminal, a waiting ambulance pulled up to the rear exit. A medic boarded and took the blanketed child in his arms. Sitting in the front, Greta and I could hear the mother's cries. It sounded so heart wrenching...sobs of pure grief.

"Please don't take him!" The mother was hysterical and wouldn't release her grip on the child.

Mr. Southwick gently pulled his wife from the medic. The couple followed him down the rear staircase and climbed into the ambulance. It raced away from the plane to the U.S. customs building and then on to the local hospital.

Feeling shaken by the sad outcome, none of us were in the mood to work the rest of the flight. But work we did. We tried to smile and be pleasant as we attended to the needs of the passengers.

Six hours later we arrived at our base in Oakland. The dispatcher told Kathy, Rike, and Heidi that they were grounded for two weeks. The child had died from spinal meningitis. Our airline wanted them at home in case they developed any symptoms from performing CPR on the sick child.

With prayers from friends, family, and crew, the three flight attendants completed their two weeks with no negative effects. Our airline released them, and they soon joined Greta and me working on another flight to Europe.

HONG KONG

After flying for a couple of years I received a one-week vacation and decided to visit Hong Kong. As we landed, I stared out the window and saw thousands of shanties a hundred feet beneath the plane's wings. Flying close to the tops of these metal shacks, I realized why Hong Kong International was considered one of the most dangerous airports in the world.

Notorious for its hazardous approach, pilots made dramatic drops down steep mountainsides and battled violent crosswinds over crowded slums. Once the wheels touched down, they immediately slammed on their brakes. The short runway covered a peninsula that protruded into Kowloon Bay, and any mistake meant landing in water.

Besides the frightening approach, my flight from Tokyo to Hong Kong was also personally daunting. As a vacationing passenger, I knew none of the crew. No one would be at the airport to greet me and my initial plans were uncertain.

On arrival I decided to spend my first night at a

top-rated hotel and then move to a youth hostel. While waiting for a customs inspector, I asked a nearby passenger, a white-haired man with a German accent, if he knew of any public transportation to the Hilton Hotel.

He replied, "My car is going right by the hotel. If you would like, I'll drop you off."

He introduced himself as Mr. Gregg and his business associate as Mr. Cutler. The three of us walked through the airport to his waiting limousine. On our ride to the hotel district I mentioned that I was an international stewardess, but that this was my first time vacationing in Hong Kong.

Mr. Gregg inquired about my evening plans and asked, "Would you like to join us for cocktails and dinner?"

"Yes, I'd enjoy that," I replied with a smile.

His driver, Yang-fu, picked me up at the Hilton's entrance about an hour later and drove me to a high-rise apartment building. He escorted me through the lavish marble lobby and waited while I cleared security. The elevator carried me to the fifth floor, and when the doors opened Mr. Gregg was there to welcome me.

His small but opulent apartment overlooked the city, and provided a pleasant retreat for him and his wife whenever they were in Hong Kong. I sat on a striped armchair near Mr. Cutler and a Chinese maid handed me a glass of wine. She wore a black uniform with a white, ruffled apron and passed a silver tray of hors d'oeuvres, bowing slightly as she handed me a linen napkin.

After a comfortable hour of visiting, Mr. Gregg said it was time to go. Sitting in the backseat of the black limo we headed into downtown Victoria, the capital of then

British-controlled Hong Kong and the center of trade, finance, and government. It was also a major destination for tourists who came to buy duty-free cameras, custom-made clothes, and jewelry.

"Why are so many people wearing pajamas?" I asked, noticing the crowds strolling on the sidewalks.

"Two or three families share one apartment. When one family sleeps, the other family either works the night shift or walks the streets," Mr. Gregg explained. "High land values create high rents. Local wages, however, are extremely low."

In due course we arrived at a well-known Mongolian restaurant. The buffet-style establishment had an unusual assortment of Asian dishes. I tried almost everything, except for the sheep's stomach lining. I also passed on anything that looked like bugs or an animal's private parts. We sat on floor cushions around a small table and ate with chopsticks while discussing local politics.

Near the end of dinner Mr. Cutler said, "I'd like to turn in early. I've had a long day of traveling, and we have an important meeting tomorrow morning."

"Bobbi, do you want to see more of Hong Kong?" Mr. Gregg asked.

"If you have time, sure," I answered.

After dropping Mr. Cutler at the apartment building, we continued around the island, stopping to visit the Floating City in Aberdeen Harbor. Almost a million people lived in this city, inhabiting homes erected from small barges. A water taxi propelled us from the mainland to a restaurant ship near the middle of the harbor.

The ship, decorated with countless white lights on its railings and riggings, looked like a Christmas ornament.

Their reflections shimmered across the waves. After a brief time at the circular bar, Mr. Gregg suggested we see Hong Kong from atop Victoria Peak.

The ride up the mountain, narrow and twisting, was too dark and obscured by trees to offer any view. Once we reached the summit, however, the scene was spectacular.

While Yang-fu waited, Mr. Gregg escorted me to a rock face high above the city. We sat on a bench and surveyed the breathtaking view before us: the sparkling lights, the boat-filled waters, and the surrounding mountains. Slowly, he put his arm around me and pulled me closer.

Mr. Gregg clearly had romantic intentions, and I, in my innocence, had been oblivious. Sitting next to a relative stranger in a foreign country, I panicked and burst into tears.

"What's wrong?" he asked.

"I have cancer," I said, crying even harder. "I only have a few months to live. That's why I'm traveling."

A few years earlier I had had a cancer scare. Needing to improvise, it was the first thing that popped into my mind.

He arose, took my arm, and gently led me back to the car. We continued down the mountainside while he patted my hand and wished me luck with my health.

When Mr. Gregg dropped me off at the Hilton, he asked, "Would you like to have my limo for a few days? I'm leaving tomorrow and would enjoy doing that for you."

"Really? Thank you very much."

The next morning, Yang-fu arrived at the hotel as instructed and we drove north to the Chinese border. I couldn't believe my good luck. Here I was, traveling on a shoestring, and I had been given a chauffeured limousine to use for sightseeing. Along the way I saw a young hitchhiker by the road and requested Yang-fu to stop.

"Where're you going?" I asked.

"Anywhere you are," he answered and tossed in his backpack. For the next few hours I had the company of Jim Bronson, a sandy-haired Canadian, and together we toured the farmlands of Hong Kong.

From our passing car we saw only women field workers. They wore loose-fitting khaki tops with pants that billowed in the breeze. On their heads were large-brimmed, pointed straw hats. They squatted as they harvested the crops, chopping sideways with their sharp sickles. Most vegetables and flowers for Hong Kong's population grew in this flat land near the Chinese border.

Returning to the south, we spotted metal and wood shacks everywhere...on steep hillsides, in gullies, and under bridges. Their tightly packed roofs overlapped each other, yet provided minimum shelter from the unrelenting monsoon rains. This was the dense mountainside slum of Kowloon that I had flown over when my plane first approached Kai Tak Airport.

Yang-fu dropped us off at an open-air market, and we spent an hour crushed between crowds of customers who, like us, were inspecting vegetables, fish, and poultry. Jim and I stood out because of our height and light hair, but otherwise we blended with the other shoppers, all wearing Western clothes. We negotiated easily, as Hong Kong's official languages are both English and Chinese.

We took the ferry from Kowloon to Victoria, the normal mode of crossing for thousands of harbor commuters. Leaning on the rails, Jim and I looked across the bay and saw several sailing ships, known as junks. Designed over a thousand years earlier, they had sectioned hulls and paneled sails. Consequently, junks were resistant to cloth and hull ruptures and could sail safely over ocean seas. For centuries, Hong Kong junks transported goods from one country to another throughout all the lands of Asia.

I checked out of the Hilton Hotel and transferred to Jim's youth hostel. I thanked Yang-fu, gave him a few dollars, and released him from his service. Jim and I later met on the inn's veranda and several guests joined us for dinner. They wanted to know why we had arrived in a limousine. I told them about the awkward situation with Mr. Gregg.

With much laughter, they marveled at my story: "You could have been raped or killed. Instead, you end up with a chauffeured limousine. Boy, an angel's watching over you."

After a few days of sightseeing and shopping in Hong Kong, I said good-bye to my newfound friends and flew back to the States.

JAPANESE BLOSSOMS AND EROTIC ART

"You lucky dogs! You'll be staying in Tokyo with the passengers for five days," the dispatcher declared. "They'll continue to Bangkok, and you'll resume a flight to Saigon before flying home."

Our crew had assembled at the Oakland base and heard the news of our two-week schedule. For most flights to Japan we landed at Tachikawa Air Base, twenty miles west of Tokyo, and received only a two- or three-day layover. This Asian trip allowed extra time for those of us who liked to shop and explore.

"You'll be staying downtown at the Imperial Hotel," the dispatcher continued.

"You've got to be kidding," I said. "That's one of the best hotels in the world."

I knew many historic facts about the hotel from my college architecture classes. It was designed by Frank Lloyd Wright and constructed in the early 1920s. To stay at the Imperial would be awesome.

After we landed in Tokyo and drove to the Imperial

Hotel, we passed a reflecting pool and continued up the driveway to the low-slanted, copper-roofed building. Uniformed men with white gloves took our luggage and led us into the reception area. The impressive interior of high ceilings, yellow-glass lamps, and built-in furniture epitomized Wright's arts and crafts design.

The passengers arrived by bus and were similarly escorted into the lobby. Our airline booked the crew on the ground floor of a three-story wing, and Elaine and I shared a room. We slept at least ten hours, recuperating from our twenty-hour duty that began in Los Angeles the previous day.

The hotel stood near the grounds of the Emperor's Imperial Palace and was walking distance to the Ginza, the main shopping area of Tokyo. It was springtime, and the cherry blossoms bloomed throughout the city. When we left the building it looked like we were strolling in a cotton-candy land.

Tokyo's police, in dark uniforms and white gloves, wore facemasks because of the city's heavy air pollution. The smog was so thick that I never saw the sun during this particular time in Japan.

At every department store, two young, uniformed girls, again with white gloves, greeted us as we entered the main doors. They bowed and lowered their eyes.

"Konnichiwa," they said. *Good afternoon.*

More girls stood at the sides of the escalators. They wiped the sliding handrails with a thick cloth and bowed another greeting as we stepped onto the moving staircase.

"I'd like to buy a kimono," I said to one of the store clerks standing on the second floor.

She escorted Elaine and me to a specific area at the

top of the third escalator. An attendant showed us a brightly colored silk kimono patterned with birds and flowers. The T-shaped robes reached the floor and had wide sleeves. The kimono's two-foot sleeves are used to store items that Western women carry in their purses.

The silk kimono I chose to buy cost thousands of dollars. Reconsidering, I picked out a blue polyester kimono decorated with pink cherry blossoms. Its price was still pretty steep…a hundred dollars. It included two belts, some tabis (a pair of two-toed socks), and a brocaded obi (the square sash at the back of the kimono).

Once the purchase was completed, we took an elevator down to the street level. Elaine and I were the last to enter and turned to face the doors. Glancing to the side, I couldn't help but notice that each generation of Japanese was defined by their height. The grandparents were small and stooped. The parents were a little taller. And the children were our height. When the doors opened, the men behind us literally pushed Elaine and me to the side so they could exit before us. Thus we learned another Japanese custom: men come first.

After shopping, Elaine and I walked to a restaurant located on a side street near the Ginza. The paved alley slanted toward the middle, where an open sewer ran. We smelled only a hint of odor, so I assumed the liquid in the center channel was mostly gray water. We learned later that Japanese farmers used human waste to fertilize their crops.

Elaine and I stopped at a tiny café. We passed under foot-long strips of navy cloth and stepped into a four-table lunch shop. To help foreigners, there were photographs of different menu dishes at the entrance. We pointed to our choice of food, notified the waitress, and ate with chopsticks, our only utensils.

Back at the hotel, we each ordered a massage. Two small girls arrived at our room and informed us through sign language about their techniques. They did not know English, and we knew just the basics of Japanese. For six dollars, they massaged our bodies for an hour.

After much rubbing, I rearranged my body so the masseuse could walk on my back. With her heels on my ribs, she curled her toes around my spine and gave me a deep massage to those muscles closest to the center. She also walked along my spine, cracking her way from my waist to my neck.

The next day Elaine and I took a public train to several tourist sites. The cleanliness, speed, and reliability of Japan's transportation system were thoroughly impressive as we traveled through the different sections of Tokyo.

Even privately owned automobiles were fastidiously clean. At every stoplight drivers got out and wiped their cars with two-foot-long feather dusters. Because of the massive destruction from World War II bombings, reconstruction was still taking place twenty-four hours a day and dust accumulated on everything.

Not wanting to squander all our layover time shopping, Elaine and I attended a class at the Imperial Hotel on woodblock printing. A design was carved on a block of wood, painted one specific color, and pressed into the paper to create a beautiful image. Another block was carved to create another layer of color. Some prints required fifty blocks of wood to produce the many subtle shades appearing in the final image.

Another class explained the rudiments of an abacus, a rectangular frame with ten or more rods, each holding numerous hollow beads. To establish a number, the user would slide the beads up and down on a dowel.

"It's faster than an adding machine," the instructor told us.

Using this unique mathematical tool, I taught the other flight attendants to calculate their monthly earnings. We were amazed by its accuracy and speed, and, surprisingly, we quickly learned how to use it.

On the last day of our layover, Elaine and I visited the Tokyo National Museum, the oldest and largest in Japan. As an art history major, I was most impressed by the paintings of ancient Japanese life. My favorite works were of mountain scenes fading into the distance through waves of fog and clouds. Artists used tiny ink brushes on silk canvases; some brushes had just a single bristle.

Besides scenery paintings, we also saw depictions of royal life, religious scenes, battles, and detailed sex acts. One painting caught my eye. It showed a nude woman sitting in a basket, bent at the waist with her hands tied to her feet. Her buttocks were at the bottom of the basket and her extremities were at the top. She was being lowered over a nude man, lying below her on a table. He had an erection, and two men stood by his side.

The docent, who had accompanied us throughout the museum, explained the Edo period painting. She continued, "Because erotic or shunga art was more profitable, Japan has many such paintings — erotic, artistic, and fun, all at the same time. The woman is positioned so that the man can enter her. Once he is inside her, the two attendants carefully rotate and spin the basket."

Elaine replied, "American art books never illustrate such sexual scenes."

"The only nudity I ever saw growing up was of aborigines in *National Geographic* magazines," I added.

The docent reacted with uncertainty to our comments, covering her mouth in embarrassment.

SOUP SURPRISE

When I returned to the States, I decided to surprise some friends and my boyfriend Bob with an authentic Japanese dinner at my apartment in Twin Peaks. I had acquired the necessary bowls and costumes to perform the ritual, and was excited to show them what I had learned in the Orient.

I caught a bus to Chinatown to have my hair fixed in a traditional geisha style. After a couple of hours with a beautician, my long brown hair was wrapped in a bun high on the back of my head. Protruding from my twisted hair were tiny bells and ornaments attached to silver sticks.

When I left the salon, the smell of sandalwood hit me as I crossed Grant Avenue and entered a pet store to buy some fish. Although I wore Western clothes, my hairstyle made dinging sounds with each step I took. I picked out six minnows and requested that they be placed in a plastic bag.

The sales clerk asked, "Would you like a bowl for the fish?"

"No thanks," I answered. "They'll be eaten to-night."

She stared at me and slowly backed away.

At my apartment I dressed in my light-blue kimono and added a pair of tabis. I gazed into the mirror and thought I looked pretty authentic.

When Bob and four friends arrived, they removed their shoes and coats. In full geisha dress I helped the men put on happi coats: black, cotton, shirt-like jackets adorned with painted flowers and belted at the waist.

My kimono draped downward in the back, showing off the soft, sensual nape of my neck. The nape is very sexual to Japanese men. I'm not sure Bob noticed the curve below my hairline, but he liked my look.

"You look fabulous. What a surprise. I can't wait for dinner."

We toasted ourselves with hot sake, wine made from rice, and began the four-course dinner. At department stores in Japan place settings of five are sold because the hostess does not eat with the guests. Instead, she waits on them throughout the meal. My five guests ate with chopsticks, sitting on floor cushions in the living room. For dinner I presented rice, a fish soup, sukiyaki (beef cooked with vegetables), and yakitori (grilled poultry). Hot sake accompanied every course.

I had placed a small hibachi in the living room fireplace so I could cook and visit at the same time. The first course was a clear, spiced soup with a live minnow swimming in a small bowl. My guests let the fish flop awkwardly on the back of their tongues for a few seconds before swallowing.

"That was interesting," Bob remarked. "Squirming

objects in my mouth, however, are probably not my favorite food choice."

Nevertheless, my Japanese dinner was a success. We all had a wonderful time with lots of laughter and lots of sake. However, no one suggested we make arrangements for another. This was definitely a once-in-a-lifetime meal.

DINNER DISASTER

"Welcome aboard," I said, smiling at the bottom of the ramp stairs. We greeted a group of sales representatives and their wives from the Ford Motor Company.

We wore fitted Polynesian muumuus on all our nonmilitary flights to Hawaii. The full-length dresses were printed with bright flowers, snug, and tied in the back. They were slit high on the sides and were considered quite risqué for the time.

From the West Coast it took over five hours to reach Honolulu. After the captain turned off the seatbelt sign, we started the requested first class service. I was assigned to the rear galley and wore an apron over my muumuu.

Once Margie and Wanda returned with finished meals, I scraped garbage into a bin and placed the trays back into their metal containers. Next, I started a beverage service. Throughout this process in the tiny kitchen, I swiveled from ovens to tray bins to coffee pots. I couldn't slow down for a second.

The airline coffee bags, made of flimsy cotton, were

located high above the coffee maker. In my rush I reached for a bag and accidentally dropped it. It struck my shoulder and burst open. Coffee grinds spilled down the front and back of my muumuu.

There was no way I could continue working with the sand-like particles scratching the skin between my breasts and down my back.

"I'll work the galley," Wanda said. "You get changed."

In the lavatory I tried to shake out the coffee grinds, but to no avail. I latched the door and took off my muumuu. I had bits of coffee in my bra and even in my panties. Double-checking the locked door, I stripped completely. I wiped my bare body and shook out my clothes, removing all traces of coffee.

While in the lavatory and still nude, I used the toilet. With typical multi-tasking competence, I wiped off the counter and basin with a paper towel while sitting on the commode. I then attempted to put the dirty towel in the overflowing garbage receptacle, but it was too full.

With force, I shoved it into the container. In doing so, I hit a sealed airsickness bag which literally exploded. Vomit struck me in the chest and I was covered from neck to belly with regurgitated food.

"SHIT! SHIT! SHIT!" I screamed.

I cleaned myself as best I could, trying not to gag. Even with lots of soap and water, I still smelled like curdled milk. Opening the door just a crack, for I was still nude, I asked Margie for the bug spray.

"What happened? We're still cleaning."

"I'll explain later," I answered. "Just hand me the spray can."

U. S. Agriculture regulations require all aircraft that land in Hawaii to be bug-sprayed, thus preventing any imported insects from ruining the state's crops. The spray had a sweet metallic odor, but it was much better than the smell of a sour stomach.

After I emerged from the bathroom, Wanda and Margie wanted to know what took me so long. When I explained, they howled with laughter. They couldn't wait to tell the others. I made them swear not to mention it to the cockpit, but I don't think they kept their promise. After we reached Hawaii, the navigator smiled and held his nose whenever he passed me on the beach.

HAWAIIAN SHERBET SHOCKER

Bob telephoned to say he had a court case in Honolulu the following week.

"Will you be there?" he asked.

As it turned out, my schedule had me in Hawaii on the exact same days.

"Let's go to Michel's," he suggested. "It's a French restaurant, and we'll be able to see a fabulous sunset from the dining room."

"Thanks, I'd love it." I smiled, thinking of another dreamy evening with Bob.

"However," he cautioned, "it's very fancy and you should dress up." He added, "Let's try to be on our best behavior."

Gee, that was rude. Did he think I would do something to embarrass him? Well, yes. That's exactly what he thought.

There was a twelve-year age difference between Bob and me. I sometimes felt like Eliza Doolittle in *My Fair Lady*. As a member of numerous Bay Area clubs, Bob taught me the nuances of San Francisco society. We sailed, skied, hiked, and partied with the third-generation offspring of some of California's most prosperous pioneers. He encouraged me to discover new activities and not to be intimidated by other people's prejudices.

Because we had dated a couple of years, I asked my gynecologist to write a prescription for birth control pills. I had no desire to get pregnant. In the 1960s I would lose my job if I married. The doctor refused to give me a prescription and instead gave me a lecture about flight attendants having sex with pilots. She had been influenced by media advertisements. She didn't know we went to them for advice, not dates.

This was before the sexual revolution of Woodstock and Haight-Ashbury. Carol Doda had just come on the scene at the Condor Club on Broadway. I was humiliated by the doctor's insinuation that I had bad morals and left her office in tears.

A week later, Bob and I were both in Honolulu. He picked me up at the Ilikai Hotel and we drove to Michel's, a four-star restaurant with blue awnings across its facade.

I wore a body-hugging black dress, cut low in the front with bold flowers etched across the bodice. Bob looked handsome in his navy sports jacket and gray slacks. Ties were required at Michel's, and he wore a conservative one with angled stripes. We passed under the arched awnings, our arms wrapped together, and stepped into the most romantic restaurant in all of Hawaii.

The maitre d' showed us to our table and customers turned to inspect the new arrivals. I felt uncomfortably scrutinized, for Bob and I were frequently confused as a father-daughter couple. What would my high school friends say? Would my dad approve? Still immature, I felt unduly anxious about other people's judgments.

Michel's French atmosphere eased my concerns. Crystal chandeliers and gilded mirrors decorated the interior, while sparkling goblets adorned the tables draped in white. The linen was placed at an angle and exotic orchids filled small vases, creating a tropical/continental setting.

We sat next to a large window overlooking Waikiki Bay and I relaxed, relishing the romantic ambiance. The waiter, dressed in a black tuxedo, presented our menus and placed white napkins on our laps with a flourish.

Bob ordered Wild Turkey on the rocks and a plate of hors d'oeuvres. I asked for a glass of chardonnay. He leaned forward, pressing his hands into mine, and we watched the setting sun transform the sky from subtle pink to an intense gold.

The waiter brought a fruit salad, and then paused before serving the main course of mahi-mahi stuffed with creamed crab. The chardonnay went well with dinner and I ordered another glass. It wasn't long before wine filled my head and I felt a little tipsy.

Not being much of a drinker, I opted to forgo an after-dinner cocktail. Instead, I chose a bright orange mango sherbet whisked with egg whites. It arrived in a silver bowl encircled by Hawaiian flowers.

I looked adoringly at Bob and took another scoop of sherbet. I don't know how it happened, but I accidentally turned the spoon over before it reached my mouth. The sherbet hit my chest and plunged down the "V" of my dress.

Bob watched in horror as the orange ball completed its downward spiral. I grabbed the napkin in my lap and pushed it into the hollow between my breasts. But in my haste I accidentally seized a corner of the tablecloth. As I shoved it down my dress, our goblets tipped over and wine splashed across Bob's crotch. He immediately rose, knocking his chair over.

Everyone turned to look, and I froze, a tablecloth protruding from my cleavage. I quickly pulled it out while Bob wiped off his slacks. Ignoring the stares, he firmly guided me toward the front door.

TURBULENCE

Turbulence is often unexpected. It can occur in clear weather, and radar can't detect it. It's the leading cause of injury for both passengers and crew. Many passengers are injured on flights because they don't have their seatbelts buckled.

Almost all flights experience some light turbulence. Passengers might strain against their seat belts. Unsecured items might fall to the floor. It's so common that most people just hang on to their trays or continue reading. The flight attendants can easily walk the aisles, and the captain may or may not illuminate the "fasten seat belt" sign.

During moderate turbulence the captain instructs the flight attendants to return to their seats. Meal services are suspended and the galley is locked down. At this point, drinks and food can easily spill. Walking is difficult. The cabin crew, however, still checks that seatbelts have been fastened.

Severe turbulence usually happens when flying through thunderclouds. No one is allowed to leave their seats and flight attendants are instructed to stay buckled. On one of my flights, while Susan and I were fastened in the rear jump seats, deafening noise from the shaking plane overwhelmed us.

A passenger panicked and rang his call button. I saw the light brighten and awkwardly left my seat and walked up the aisle.

"What's wrong?" I asked when I reached the illuminated light.

"I think I'm having a heart attack," the elderly man said as he rubbed his chest.

"Give me a moment," I said, clutching the armrest with one hand and loosening his tie with the other. "I'll be right back."

As I returned to the rear I gripped passenger seat tops, trying to keep my balance. The nearest oxygen bottle was in the overhead rack by the aft galley.

"Throw me some wet towels," I yelled to Rike.

"You shouldn't be standing," she scolded.

I kicked off my shoe, stepped up onto a seat, and unstrapped the oxygen bottle. Clutching the heavy weight against my body, I let go of the overhead frame to step down. At that instant the plane pitched down and plummeted at least a hundred feet. For a second or so I floated, suspended in air.

If I hadn't had the heavy bottle clutched to my chest, I would have cracked my head against the cabin ceiling. I toppled to the floor, regained my composure, and caught the towels Rike threw. With a struggle I returned to the ailing passenger.

I placed a mask over his nose and mouth as I sat tightly buckled in the seat alongside. Patting his forehead with damp towels, I said, "We'll be out of this shortly. Don't worry." Before long he calmed down, and so did our plane.

Administering oxygen was quite common in those early years of jet travel. First-time passengers often suffered anxiety attacks. During the severe turbulence on this particular flight, we were lucky to have only one passenger needing oxygen.

The fourth level of turbulence is called "extreme." In eight years of international travel I never flew in extreme turbulence. It's exceptionally rare. It's like flying through a tornado.

On the most turbulent flight I ever experienced, strong winds hit us before we had even left Oakland. After the gate agent shut the door, the Boeing started to shake and rocked sideways as a tractor pushed the jet away from the terminal toward the taxiway.

Our passengers were a group of revelers intent on having a week on the sunny shores of Waikiki. The flight attendants started a liquor service as soon as we reached cruising altitude. With drinks and snacks on trays, the plane continued to shudder.

"Fasten your seat belts and keep them tight," the captain announced over the PA system. "Flight attendants. Secure the galley and stay seated until I tell you otherwise."

In the tossing plane, Leigh and I quickly checked the passengers for seatbelt compliance. Susan slammed and locked galley cabinet doors and stashed supplies. We returned to our seats and pulled our belts tight.

For the next four hours the infamous Hawaiian trade winds battered our plane. Susan and I were thrown about like sock puppets against our seat straps. We fell to the right, and seconds late were hurled to the left.

The pitching became so erratic there was no chance to read. Words on a page bounced all over. We just had to sit with our backs to the aft wall and watch the passengers lurch from side to side in front of us. To kill time, we forced ourselves to talk.

"My teeth are chattering," I said.

"I feel sick," Susan responded.

"My ears popped," I countered.

Gravity tore at every loose item. Pillows and blankets flew from the overhead racks. Books and magazines were tossed to the ceiling and then fell to the floor. Periodically we were in a state of weightlessness. The trashed cabin looked like a jungle of junk.

The brutal pitches continued for the next few hours. For the first time in my airline career I feared for our plane's ability to fly. As the wind cruelly chucked our plane, cold chills rolled down my back.

"Please, Lord," I prayed. "Don't let us crash."

The 707 rammed into a massive column of rising air. The trembling plane was flung upwards, and then suddenly dropped a couple hundred feet. Though belted into our seats, our bodies slammed backwards with every violent vibration, and people screamed whenever we experienced an exceptionally strong jolt.

As the winds thundered against the sides of the jet, we heard the sounds of retching and worried about a chain reaction. And sure enough, everyone began throwing up. Vomit smell clouded the rear of the plane and a wave of nausea rolled through my stomach. It took all my willpower not to follow suit.

Four hours later, when we approached Honolulu, the worst of the terror was over. It looked like a twister had touched down in the cabin. Anything not locked or attached was thrown about: shoes, purses, books, pillows, hats, and magazines.

The plane landed smoothly, and the passengers clapped and cheered. After they had gathered their belongings, they wobbled toward the exit. We followed them, shaking our heads in amazement at the mess in the cabin. Thank goodness we had a few days to rest before working another flight back to the States.

MY BABY'S NOT BREATHING!

Our flight left Boston fifteen minutes after the scheduled departure time. Our airline was taking another group of sightseers to the British Isles.

With many families and numerous children on board, Nancy and I had our hands occupied filling baby bottles, handing out junior wings, and entertaining youngsters bored during the six-hour flight.

"Can you help me?" a young mother asked as I walked toward my station in the rear of the plane.

Her toddler was crying and trying to escape her grasp.

"Here, try this," I said, handing her some paper doilies and a crayon. The boy immediately became occupied with drawing and stopped squirming.

"I'll bring you some juice. That should help."

While I was going about my duties, Amy, a ten-year-old with blond braids, followed me. She wore a blue pastel dress with white lace around the collar.

She and her parents were going to visit their extended family in Ireland. Throughout the flight she tugged at my skirt and asked never-ending questions.

"Why do we have to put seat backs and tray tables up?"

"Because, Amy," I answered, "in an emergency the seatbacks and tables can hinder passengers from leaving."

"Why do you want us to have our window shades open when we land?"

"Again, Amy, in case of an emergency it helps the rescuers see inside."

She was obviously very smart. I let her wear an extra uniform smock and added junior wings to the outfit. She loved being a little flight attendant, and her parents were thankful for the attention she received.

After the dinner service Amy fell asleep and I returned to the back of the plane to continue my chores. Nancy finished cleaning the aft galley while I stocked supplies in the lavatories.

Finally, we sat down to enjoy our own meals. Nancy and I parked next to each other on the wide jump seat and chatted as we ate.

A young man approached the rear area. He didn't interrupt our conversation and never said a word. He just stood there and looked at us. I thought he was waiting for one of the restrooms.

"They're not occupied," I said. "Just open the door."

He murmured, "My baby's not breathing."

He said the words so calmly that they didn't seem real. I quickly placed my tray in the galley and followed him to his seat. His teenage wife was cradling a limp baby, tears falling down her face as she rocked back and forth.

Hearing her husband's voice, she looked up.

"What's wrong with your baby?" I asked.

She couldn't answer and kept crying.

"Please, give me the baby. Let me check."

Hesitantly, she handed the two-month-old infant to me. I held him in front of me and looked in his mouth. I shook him lightly. No response.

I turned him over and hit him firmly in the center of his back. Again, no reaction. I turned him face down for a second time and solidly struck him between his shoulder blades. I smacked him so hard I feared I might have broken some bones.

All of a sudden the infant let out a piercing scream and started crying. The parents joined in, but these were cries of happiness. I held the baby for another minute and checked his back and mouth. Everything seemed to be in good order, so I returned him to his mother.

She embraced the infant, supporting him in the crook of her arm, and gave him a bottle of milk. The father shook my hands and thanked me profusely. He stayed in the aisle, lit a cigarette, and inhaled deeply. I think he had been holding his breath the whole time I held his son.

If the infant had not responded, I would have raced with him to the rear of the plane, starting mouth-to-mouth resuscitation along the way. Nancy would have begun heart palpitations on the baby while I continued forcing air into his lungs.

Since we were over the Atlantic Ocean, it would have been a couple of hours before we could have made an emergency landing. Thank goodness the infant's blocked airway opened.

A tragedy had been diverted. I was shaking from

both happiness and fear. Nancy and I smiled and cried, hugging each other and thanking God for His help. Amy appeared and stared at us.

"Why are you crying?"

I explained that we had just saved a baby from a tummy ache. She was incredulous.

"My mom doesn't cry when I get a tummy ache," she said.

"Come. Help Nancy clean the galley," I said. "I have to go up front."

I was unsettled when I entered the cockpit and reported the incident. The senior flight attendant recorded the names of the infant and parents, the details of the baby's non-response, and the subsequent result.

Although I never saw an object expelled from the baby's mouth, I suggested a blocked airway. At that time SIDS, or Sudden Infant Death Syndrome, was barely known to the general public. In retrospect, that might have been the reason for the child's inability to wake up.

The next couple of hours were a fog to me. Amy followed me everywhere, but my mind kept going back to the infant and how I had responded. Did I perform as we had been instructed? What else could have been done?

Finally, we landed in Shannon. I stood at the bottom of the rear ramp, thanking everyone for flying with us. Amy came down the stairs, proudly wearing her junior wings and beaming from ear to ear.

Soon after, the infant's parents deplaned and we warmly embraced. Our airline had medical personnel waiting for them; their baby would be thoroughly checked before they could continue their travels.

Yes, it was a beautiful day in Ireland.

AMSTERDAM'S LITTLE BO PEEP

Later that autumn, the scheduling department assigned Connie, Robin, and me to fly for the next few weeks between the East Coast and Europe. The first part of the trip we worked a flight from JFK to Amsterdam, where we enjoyed a three-day layover in the Netherlands's capital city.

"Hey, let's get some culture," I said.

"I want to see the Dutch Masters," Robin responded. As a fine arts painter, she often encouraged us to visit museums during our layovers.

"And I want to see Anne Frank's house," said Connie, a substitute teacher on her off days.

The three of us hired a taxi and toured the historic Rijksmuseum, the national museum. Rembrandt and Vermeer were some of the Old Masters whose paintings were on display. Van Gogh was represented among the Impressionists. It was a dream comes true for Robin. She took notes and informed us about painting details and odd brush strokes.

From there we took a bus to Anne Frank's house. We learned that the teenager, her father, mother, sister, and four other Jewish people hid in a five-hundred-square-foot attic for over two years. The staircase to the attic was hidden behind a small revolving bookcase, which looked like all the others in the house. Because she never left the attic during this period, Anne's only connection to the outside world was looking upward through a skylight. She saw birds and a chestnut tree and wrote about them in her diary.

While on the grounds of the house looking at the famous tree, we chatted with other young tourists. They told us about another place we should visit.

"The Erotic Museum displays art and artifacts," one said. "The history of sex in Europe is really interesting."

We took another bus, this time to the center of the oldest section of the city. De Wallen is a wide street divided by a canal and located in the red-light district. On each side of the canal were three-story buildings with large display windows on the middle floors.

Prostitution is legal and regulated in Amsterdam. The country has allowed and taxed brothels since the 1500s. The windows displayed the women whose attributes were for sale. They wore accessories emphasizing their specialties: whips and chains, toddler clothes, short skirts with spiked heels.

We crossed a stone bridge and found the museum on the other side of the canal. To enter, we had to step through a gigantic vagina, complete with foot-long pubic hair around the sides. Once indoors, a docent greeted us. She explained the numerous artifacts displayed in the glass case near the front door. There were penises in many sizes and colors, mock-ups of women's private parts and condoms in all shapes and material.

From the main room, we moved to a small movie theatre that smelled of cigarettes and marijuana. There were only a dozen upholstered seats in the dark room. We watched an erotic version of the cartoon *Snow White and the Seven Dwarfs*. Although no ratings existed, it must have been XXXX. To the music of "Whistle While You Work," Snow White performed oral sex on the seven little men. To say the least, this was quite a surprise for Robin, Connie, and me.

We left the theatre, passing hundreds of bicycles, and strolled back to the windowed apartments.

"Hi. What are you doing here?" asked a young U.S. soldier who approached us on the other side of the canal.

"The same thing you are," I said. "Sightseeing."

The soldier's name was Steve. He was standing next to a tree with another soldier named Paul. We learned that Jim, a third soldier, had left to experience one of the hookers. He had chosen the cute one with boots and a cowboy hat.

As we chatted, the five of us stood a few feet in front of a window exhibiting a woman dressed like Little Bo Peep, complete with a shepherd's hook. She waved to us from the window and we waved back. Before long she came out to the landing and beckoned to us, yelling something in Dutch.

"What does she want?" I asked.

"She accepts women," Paul guessed.

"No way!" Connie exclaimed.

We returned to talking, our backs to the woman in the window. In a few moments I saw Bo Peep walking toward us. Her angry eyes were like olives, black and bulging; and she carried a gray bucket in her hand. I watched in horror as she hurled the contents toward our little group.

Robin received the worst of it. She was drenched from head to toe.

"Holy shit!" she screamed. "What happened? What is this?"

Fearing the bucket might have contained urine, Robin mopped madly at her face and hair. We panicked and rushed to her rescue.

Once we realized it was only water, we erupted in laughter. We now understood the prostitute's waving. If we weren't going to be customers, she wanted us to leave her territory.

Jim soon returned and stared at the five of us, still hooting and hollering.

"What's going on?"

Then he looked at Robin.

"What happened to you?"

We were laughing so hard we could barely explain. After the hysterics abated, we said our good-byes and walked to a taxi stand.

What a day we had. We started out viewing some of the best paintings in the world and ended up in the red-light district, being attacked by a prostitute.

A "BROKEN" LEG

My airline prohibited its employees from taking extended vacations. In 1967 I had requested a four-month leave of absence and it had been denied. I was only given two weeks of vacation. Consequently, I improvised.

I convinced Carole, my roommate, to ask a fellow hospital colleague to wrap my leg in a cast.

"Once the photos are taken, I'll mail them to World Airways from Bangkok, explaining that I had an accident while on vacation," I said. "They certainly can't expect me to return to work with a broken leg."

We drove to the hospital and met a doctor who applied gauze and a plaster cast while I sat on an emergency room table. He loaned me crutches and I had photos taken to verify my "accident." Now we were ready to go home and party.

Balloons and travel posters decorated our apartment. Beer and wine flowed along with sourdough bread and Dungeness crab. What could be better! I tried to sing "These Boots Are Made for Walking," but I could only stumble between our guests. We laughed, told stories, and everyone signed their names on my cast.

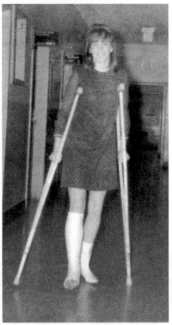

A "broken" leg

As midnight approached the partiers left with kisses and hugs, and my roommates disappeared into their bedrooms. Making my drunken way to the bathroom, I filled a tub full of hot, soapy water and got in—cast and all. In my inebriated state I enjoyed the first few minutes in the bath, and then reality hit.

No one had informed me how to remove the cast. I assumed I could soak if off, since it had just been put on.

Wrong! I sat in the tub for so long my skin began to crease and turn purple.

I pulled and tugged, but the cumbersome blob would not break free. I took a hammer and slammed the cast so hard I thought I had actually broken it—the leg, that is. The cast was still there.

With tears in my eyes, I hobbled nude to the kitchen. The party had ended, everyone had left, and a hangover headache had started. This was definitely not one of my better ideas.

Rummaging through drawers, I found some heavy-duty shears and attempted to cut off the cast. Sitting on the floor, I cut and tore at the tough fibers. Finally, two hours after the party had ended, the cast came off and I staggered back to my bedroom.

The next day was a blur. Thank goodness I had packed earlier in the week. My standard outfit for traveling was a navy chiffon dress, hemmed above my knees. It was classy, easy to wash, and didn't wrinkle. There was always a chance that I could be bumped up to first class and I wanted to fit the part.

I said goodbye to my roommates, and Bob drove me to the airport. With kisses and tears, we parted.

"I can't believe you're actually leaving," Bob said. "Write often. I'll miss you."

I walked into the Oakland terminal to begin the first leg of my trip, flying to Japan on my airline. In Tokyo I mailed the photo of me in a cast to World Airways and asked for an extension to my vacation. For the next six weeks I flew as a passenger on Lufthansa, sightseeing in Thailand, India, Pakistan, and Egypt.

AN INTERLUDE IN CAIRO

As the plane touched down in Cairo, I looked at my watch. It was 5 a.m. on Saturday, June 2, 1967.

When we landed, only two other passengers disembarked. They were both reporters for a Los Angeles newspaper. We walked across the tarmac into a three-story building.

"Gosh, no one is here," I murmured.

It was strange that there were no employees or any other passengers present in this gigantic international airport. Having had no access to news for the past few weeks, I guessed it was because we had arrived so early in the morning.

Finally, an official came and processed the three of us. He barely looked through my two suitcases before pointing to a Hilton shuttle car outside the main doors. My normal traveling procedure was to go to a top-rated hotel the initial night and get my bearings. Afterwards I would transfer to a youth hostel.

The Hilton had lush landscaping in all shades

of green, with elaborate fountains and tall palm trees in front of the high building. My room, with tiled floors and contemporary furniture, was on the eighth floor and overlooked parts of the bustling city. After a short nap I did my laundry and immediately changed the décor to modern hippie, hanging wet clothes everywhere.

From the hotel, I strolled to the nearby American Express office. In the sixties this was the place to pick up mail and meet other travelers. On my way there I viewed an array of boarded-up shops. Piles of sandbags were placed in front of the doors. Very few people were on the streets and virtually no women.

When I arrived at the AE office, the front door was open. No one was around. No young people reading their mail, no employees standing behind the counters. I shouted "hello," trying to rouse someone to help me. With no answer, I walked down the narrow hallway to the rear offices, calling "hello" as I went along. Finally I came to an open office and saw a middle-aged man sitting behind a desk, bent over a pile of papers.

I introduced myself and asked, "Where is everyone?"

"What the hell are you doing here?"

Shocked by his abrupt manner, I answered, "I'm looking for my mail."

He responded, "Egypt is closed to tourists. War is about to break out!"

Once I clarified that I had just arrived that morning and had been traveling for six weeks, he calmed down. He explained that he was John Riley, the manager of the office, and said the Hilton Hotel was now the operational base for all news media, foreign diplomats, a few businessmen, and now me. Egypt had become way too dangerous. All nonessential people, even John's wife and children, had been sent home.

"You are not to be alone on the streets at any time," he warned and escorted me back to the hotel. When we returned to the Hilton, John introduced me to the hotel manager, Hank Adler.

"Bobbi's by herself. Please look after her until it's safe for her to leave Egypt," he requested.

What luck! Hank was in his early thirties, originally from Austria, and fluent in half a dozen languages. He was about six feet tall with dark brown hair, and drop-dead gorgeous. If I had to be looked after by someone, this was the person I definitely would have chosen.

Hank said, "Although our country is on alert, we go about our daily routines as much as possible. I'm going sailing in a few minutes. Want to join me?"

"Great. I'd love that."

His boat was close by and for a couple of hours we sailed up and down the Nile. The late afternoon sky was an unbroken expanse of blue and the day became quite hot. I was lying on my stomach on the forward platform in my white-dotted bikini, sunning myself. Raising my head, I watched the landscape change from city to farmland.

Hank clearly took "looking after me" to heart. The next day he invited me to an unusual Egyptian restaurant. It was a few miles from the streets of Giza, across the Nile from Cairo, out in the barren desert. Customers had to arrive by camel or horse.

We rode with English saddles and bridles and paced our way from the outskirts of Giza into the nearby desert. The land was flat. No dunes in sight. Our horses walked and cantered most of the way along the hard-packed sand.

When we came upon the restaurant, I was astonished to see a huge, circus-like tent, possibly three-stories high, standing by itself in the middle of the sandscape. A few horses, camels, and their assigned attendants were stationed at one side. After we dismounted, two men in starched uniforms emerged, holding the tent flaps aside for us to enter. We were greeted by many employees, who all seemed to know Hank.

"Welcome, Mr. Adler," they murmured, bowing slightly as he passed.

Our table was a mat on a carpeted floor, surrounded by hand-woven pillows. Spoons and fingers were our utensils as we sat cross-legged on the cushions. In this elaborate atmosphere of gilded chandeliers and oriental carpets, we were the only customers.

While we ate, we were entertained by piercing music coming from a small orchestra in the rear of the tent. Soon a barefoot teenage girl, dressed in a turquoise outfit, began dancing for us. The diaphanous pants had silver beads and coins attached, hanging from the lower part of her hips. The short top covered her shoulders and stopped below her breasts, leaving her midriff bare.

She moved slowly to the music's rhythm, softly clicking finger cymbals. She seemed to be in a trance, her body arched backward, her long hair swaying. We sat looking up at her, our eyes following her every motion. It was my first time seeing a belly dancer, and her sensual, snake-like movements captivated me. Not just her stomach, but also her hands, shoulders, and neck all stirred and twisted to the sounds of the high-pitched music.

By the time we left the restaurant, darkness had

fallen. We mounted our horses and commented about the sparkling lights in the distance.

"Before we return to Cairo," Hank said, "I want to show you Egypt's *son et lumieres* program. It's a short ride from here."

In this historic play without actors, a tale was told using synchronized lights, recorded voices, and music. It was a narrative about a pharaoh who was entombed within the Great Pyramid of Giza. The two smaller pyramids once contained the bodies of other pharaohs.

Hundreds of folding chairs, perhaps even a thousand chairs, were lined in a semicircle in front of the three pyramids. Music played, and when a deep voice came over the loudspeaker one of the pyramids lit up. We sat on our horses watching the play with no one else in attendance. Except for us, the entire arena was empty.

After an hour, we headed for the stables. As we rode away from the lights of the pyramids, a small group of beggars approached us, their hands outstretched.

"Not today," Hank said, shaking his head.

One of the men grabbed the reins of Hank's horse and shouted for his men to attack. Hank raised his riding crop and smashed it over the robber's head.

"Run, Bobbi!" he yelled. "Get out of here!"

I kicked my horse and off I went. We flew from the robbers as fast as we could go, heading toward the city lights. It was incredibly dark, lit only by a waning moon. Bending over my horse's neck, I encouraged him to go faster. The dust from the dirt-like sand flew in the air. After a few tense minutes Hank caught up with me, and we continued at full speed.

Out of breath and with my heart pounding, we dismounted at the Giza stables. Our horses were covered in white sweat and breathing hard. We handed them to the grooms and Hank told them about the attempted robbery.

"Call a taxi," Hank said. "We're going back to Cairo."

The ride to the hotel was solemn and quiet. I curled up in one corner of the back seat and mulled over the dangers we had just avoided. Hank pulled me gently toward him, and I nestled into his arms. When we reached the hotel, he hugged me goodnight.

"We'll see each other tomorrow," he whispered.

WAR BREAKS OUT

That night I fell into an exhausted sleep. Hours later, earsplitting sirens awakened me. Right on the dot of nine o'clock, Monday morning, the air raids began. A hotel employee banged on my door.

"Hurry! Get dressed and follow me," he ordered.

He escorted me to an outside staircase—an open-grated fire escape. Since my room was on the eighth floor, I had to go down that many flights plus two others to reach the security of the lowest level. All the hotel guests had been sequestered in the basement. While we waited for information, we talked about the bombing we heard in the distance.

Having had no access to current events, I asked Bill McDonald, a Chicago correspondent, for an update. He told me that President Nasser and the Soviet Union had exchanged incorrect intelligence about Israel amassing troops on Syria's border. Nasser began gathering his own troops on Israel's border. To Israel, Nasser's actions were viewed as an act of war. They responded immediately with preemptive strikes at Egypt's military airfields and Cairo's international airport. That was the bombing we were hearing.

As soon as the all-clear whistle sounded, the basement crowd returned to the central part of the hotel, this time using elevators. I left with them and had just opened my room door when the telephone rang.

"Are you all right?" Hank asked.

While we were talking, another air-raid siren sounded. Once again, I was escorted to the fire escape and descended the eight plus flights to the basement. I had a fear of heights and the open-grated staircase, so many stories above the pavement, frightened me.

Once the all-clear whistle sounded for the second time, I immediately went to the front desk.

"Please change my room to a lower floor," I requested.

The clerk gave me a second floor suite and bellhops transported my luggage.

For the next two days, as the air raids sounded, the hotel guests traveled from their rooms, to the basement, and out to the hotel grounds. I never saw Hank during these hectic cycles, but he called numerous times.

The next day Bill asked, "Would you like to join us for a tour of Cairo?"

"Yes, I would."

I was eager to leave the hotel grounds as I had now been there for four days (two on my own and two as a captive). Since the bombing was at the military and Cairo airports, miles away from the Hilton, I felt completely safe. I was wedged in the backseat between two reporters while Bill sat in the front passenger seat.

He leaned around while we were driving and told

me, "Israel just destroyed Egypt's entire air force."

We hadn't been on the road for more than a few minutes when we were stopped by a checkpoint guard and asked to show our identification. Our taxi was immediately surrounded by a group of black-uniformed policemen bearing machine guns.

A young soldier scanned the inside, stopping to stare at me. I tried to look unconcerned when he asked for our documents. All the reporters had their press credentials. I had nothing.

One of the reporters slipped me his ID after he had showed it to the officer. Chills raced down my spine as I passed it to the guard. With enormous effort I steadied my shaking hand.

Thank goodness the press card had no photo on it and the guard could not read English. Although we passed the inspection, we couldn't continue and were ordered back to the hotel. I don't think I took a full breath until we were some distance from the checkpoint. Then all five of us let out a collective sigh of relief.

When we approached the Hilton, another correspondent drew near. Mike Landsky was a large man—well over six feet tall and relatively heavy. His shirt was soaked with blood. His face was covered with black and blue bruises. One eye was swollen shut, and his head was bloated like a basketball.

"What happened to you?" Bill asked.

"They saw me taking photos from that building," he said, pointing across the street. "The police caught me on the staircase."

"Then what?"

"I held the stair rails and kicked them as they rushed

me. One guy reached over and hit me with his belt. The buckle blinded me. That's when they got me."

Once they finished beating him, they confiscated his camera gear. The police dragged him back to the Hilton and dumped him at the entrance. The hotel staff cleaned his wounds, and he waited for Bill to return.

The Cairo Hilton held almost all the non-Egyptians in the country. With so many Americans and Israelis inside, the building became a target and was specifically threatened. Evacuation plans by the U.S. government were formed.

There were a total of 567 of us, which turned out to be too large a group to leave at one time. Consequently, half were ordered to take a train to the portside city of Alexandria, about 120 miles west of Cairo. The other half would stay at the Hilton and leave on the day of the rescue.

A few hours after the first half left the Hilton under escort, it was decided to send four more. This small group was made up of Jack Howard (an African-American dentist), Sven Johnson (a Swedish diplomat), Mary Clark (a Fulbright Scholar's wife, living in Alexandria), and me. I said a heartfelt good-bye to Hank and joined the other three for a cab ride to the station.

We were unusually quiet during the long train ride through the countryside. I looked at the blackness beyond the window and wondered, "What will happen next?"

TERROR IN ALEXANDRIA

It was an hour or so before midnight when we arrived in Alexandria. We hailed a taxi and Jack told the driver to take us to a hotel. We drove past crowds of yelling men who were shooting rifles into the air. Because we were non-Egyptians, none of the first few hotels we approached wanted to accept us.

Finally we found one that would admit us and we checked in at the front desk. Mary and I shared a room on the second floor, near the top of the staircase. Just as we walked into our suite, there was a huge explosion. The harbor had been bombed; and as it turned out, our hotel was located right on the waterfront.

All lights in the hotel went out, plunging us into total darkness. Having just arrived, I had no idea where to go or how to get there. I couldn't see a thing. From the adjacent corridor I could hear screaming and crying.

"Mary! Mary!" I called. "Where are you?"

I stared into the darkness, but she was nowhere to be found. With piercing noises all around and not being able to see a thing, I crawled on my hands and knees, feeling my way down the winding staircase to the first floor.

The lights flickered back on as I passed through an empty dining room. The large, vertical windows, overlooking the Mediterranean, were destroyed. Tables were vacant, chairs were knocked over, and plates were left filled with food. I had not eaten since breakfast and grabbed a piece of fried chicken. As I entered the hotel lobby, a grenade exploded outside the front windows. Glass shattered everywhere.

Hotel attendants located Sven and me and pushed us into a dark closet adjacent to the front door and locked us in. Sven was visibly shaken and fell to his knees, head buried in his hands. With the hem of my skirt I wiped the sweat from my face.

I leaned forward and peeked through a tiny gap in the door. A mob of wild men ran in from the street, shouting loudly and brandishing firearms over their heads. The hair on the back of my neck stood straight up. I was terrified.

"Please, dear Lord, protect us," I silently prayed as the minutes ticked by.

I imagined beatings and rape. What would become of me? Would I be killed? Trembling, I peered out the crack in the door and looked on in horror.

As soon as the unruly men left the lobby, a staff employee located Mary and Jack in an upstairs hallway. We were asked to check out, even though we had just checked in. We found another taxi and left immediately.

Although it was the beginning of a new day, it was still dark outside when we drove to Mary's apartment. Her building had no security employees, but she now felt it was safer than the downtown hotels. Along the way we saw countless buildings with smashed windows, cars overturned, and roadside fires.

We snuck into her lodgings, and for the next forty-eight hours the four of us stayed hidden in her two-room apartment. Although we could hear shooting in the distance and smelled burning tires, we kept the curtains drawn at all times; we never looked out.

During the day we moved quietly and whispered constantly. We slept on the floor using throw pillows and towels. No lights were allowed at any time. Mary's neighbor Mohammed slipped us food and informed us about the latest evacuation plans.

"Time to get ready," he said.

We were to leave in the middle of the night and reach the wharf region by early morning. A ship from the U.S. Navy's Sixth Fleet had just arrived. We hurriedly said good-bye to Mohammed, and silently climbed into a taxi for the long ride to Alexandria's international seaport.

On our way there we had to drive through a military base that fronted the shipyard. As the night began to fade and the day dawned, the driver cleared security and was told to stay on the main road. By doing so, we passed between hundreds of shouting troops that had assembled in a great square.

As we advanced toward the crowd, we saw a man hanging in effigy. The image, dressed in Western clothes, swung on a rope as the soldiers chanted for justice.

The driver steered deliberately and cautiously, maneuvering between the screaming men. They were so close to our taxi I could have touched them.

We scrunched our heads between our knees and

covered ourselves with our jackets. I dreaded a real hanging and smelled the sweat of fear in our cab.

I was absolutely terrified of what awaited me. My heart pounded and my head throbbed. I closed my eyes, blocking out the surrounding scene. Again, I prayed.

The taxi moved slowly, fearful of accidentally hitting one of the screaming soldiers. It seemed like hours, but finally we crossed the square. The troops, preoccupied with the hanging, ignored our vehicle.

We now had only a short distance to drive. As we approached the docks, a silver ship was outlined against the early morning sky. Above it, the Stars and Stripes blew in the wind.

"What a beautiful sight," I exclaimed.

We exited the taxi and entered the terminal. In a few hours, the U.S. Navy's Sixth Fleet transported all 567 of us across the Mediterranean to Greece. June 10th was a sunny day, not a cloud in the sky. And it was the end of the infamous Six-Day War.

MILE HIGH CLUB

"I love staying in France," I said to the other flight attendants.

Ferrying a plane to Paris was a great treat for us. Our European routes usually had us working to England or Ireland. Now we had the luxury of staying in a plush hotel in the center of the city. After a few hours of rest and reorganizing, we began to shop.

Greta, Rike, and I wore stylish dresses and high heels as we walked along the Champs-Élysée, a beautiful tree-lined avenue near the hotel. We enjoyed watching the shoppers and stopped at expensive boutiques. Rike purchased Chanel perfume and I bought Lalique glass. The dollar exchange was in our favor and we purchased them at bargain prices. We were in heaven.

After a day of shopping, we visited the nearby park and watched marionette shows—free and entertaining. The puppets moved on strings within a small, portable stage, and, of course, they spoke in French. We understood the basics without being fluent in the language.

The children standing in front of us interacted with the puppets, calling back and forth. The parents and surrounding audience laughed at the youngster's outrageous comments. Rike, Greta, and I joined the crowd in the teasing.

From the park we walked to the Arc de Triomphe and the Eiffel Tower. We acted as typical tourists and had our photos taken. When we returned to the hotel, we learned of a change in departure dates. We had to report to duty the following afternoon.

At Orly International Airport we picked up a group of French college students flying to the States. The 707 jet had plenty of empty seats, and the undergraduates spread themselves throughout the plane.

When we demonstrated the emergency procedures, they joked, laughed, and completely ignored us. They felt superior and demanded that we respond immediately to their every request. They also insisted we speak only French. As a graduate from a top university, I had a hard time being gracious to these pompous students.

After dinner and several glasses of wine, most of the students fell asleep. Greta, Rike, and I cleaned the galley and lavatories, checked the cabin, and returned to the rear to relax and eat our own dinners. Rike leaned against the galley counter while Greta and I sat on the jump seats.

"What a bunch of jerks," Greta commented. "Not one 'please' or 'thank you' from any of them."

"I agree. The Parisians were so nice, but these kids are spoiled brats."

Rike added, "Only three more hours."

The dark cabin had a few reading lights illuminated as we crossed the Atlantic. On one of my many check walks from the back galley to the front, I heard a strange sound coming from an aisle seat. It was too dark for me to see what was happening.

"Rike, will you help me? Something weird is going on," I said.

She followed me as I walked back up the aisle. Pointing a flashlight toward a row of seats, we found the source of the noise. It came from beneath an undulating blanket. A passionate couple moaned in unison, the tan blanket moving up and down. They had obviously joined the Mile High Club.

"Okay, you two. Stop and sit up," I ordered.

Rike saw the infamous third finger protruding from the cover. She ripped off their blanket and the smell of sex flooded the air.

"Sit up now!" she demanded in a loud voice. "And fasten your seat belts!"

Grumbling, they smoothed their clothes and sat up. I'm not that proficient in French, but I was pretty sure the male student was not muttering nice words as he pulled up his pants and straightened his hair.

Couples who engage in sex while flying in a plane above 5,280 feet gain membership to the Mile High Club. The thrill of not being discovered in such a public place makes joining the club exciting. But it's a sexual fantasy that rarely happens. Despite the tall tales, only a few people actually belong. And none of our crew members, as far as I knew.

While going about her normal duties, Greta noticed a male student sneak into a restroom.

"Why is he acting so suspiciously?" she asked. Before long we heard loud groans.

"Oh, no!" I exclaimed. "Not again!"

Greta banged on the door and demanded, "You come out now!"

They laughed out loud. "We are. We *are* coming!"

After a minute or so, two young men emerged, smiling and snickering.

"I don't believe it," I said to Rike and Greta.

On this one flight we witnessed two couples join the Mile High Club. In all our years of flying, we had never even seen one such event. The French obviously deserve their worldwide reputation.

MIDDLE EASTERN ETIQUETTE

Flying from France or Italy, our airline often had passengers who had originated in the Middle East and were continuing their journeys to the United States.

The women wore black robes (*abayas* or *chadors*), covering them from head to toe. The men wore European suits or white robes, some with checkered red and white headdresses.

Although the travelers were pleasant, we had problems with their lack of knowledge regarding Western toilets. In their countries, toilet facilities are nothing more than a hole surrounded by slanting tiles. A person stood with his feet on either side of the hole, squatted, and eliminated waste. Not knowing how to use airplane facilities, many stepped on top of the toilet seat and squatted.

Consequently, after a Middle Eastern person used our bathrooms, a flight attendant would have to enter and clean the footprints off the toilet seat. Sometimes we had to get on our hands and knees and scrub the floor. That happened if a passenger had used the faucet water to clean his private parts.

Standing in the rear of the airplane, I decided to teach the passengers the proper way to operate a toilet. The procedure had to be demonstrated, as they did not speak English.

I stopped a white-robed man before he entered the lavatory and through sign language asked him to watch me work the bathroom fixtures. While he stood outside looking in, I pretended to sit on the toilet seat. I stood up and guided my finger to the flush button. He reacted by quickly stepping backward, startled by the suction noise.

When I showed him that our airline objected to people washing their private parts, he shook his head in disagreement. And he really took offence to my being his instructor. Men from the Middle East gave orders. Women received them.

We had only female flight attendants on board, so I had no alternative but to stand at the sink and splash water toward the crotch of my plastic apron. Shaking my head, I said sharply to him, "No. No. No."

Eventually he understood and explained the rules to the other passengers in line. From then on the rear lavatories had a modest amount of order, and I was relieved of most of my clean-up duties. Another few hours and we'd be in New York, where their friends and family would be able to continue with the toilet instructions.

MAFIA FLIGHTS

A month later I was assigned to work a flight from New York to Las Vegas. We called them mafia flights. They were Italian gamblers who ordered first-class services. These flights occurred on a regular basis during the sixties.

As our limousine driver drove the crew from the Statler Hilton in Manhattan to the airport, the navigator flicked a cigarette butt out his window.

"That's littering," I said, surprised by my audacity.

"This is New York, they don't care," he said, gesturing to the window. "Look around. Garbage everywhere."

"It's a good thing you didn't have my mother as your parent. She would have stopped the car and make you go back and pick it up. She did that to me once when I tossed out a gum wrapper."

He turned his back to me and the conversation ended. However, he never threw anything else from the limo. I had made my point.

Before we pushed away from the terminal, the flight attendants gave out candy and five-cigarette packs to the passengers. The men wore suits with open-collared shirts, flaunting their gold chains. We folded fur coats and placed them in the overhead compartments.

Once we were airborne, we passed out steaming towels perfumed with lemon. Next we served two miniature bottles of liquor and hot hors d'oeuvres. Nothing was missing from these first-class flights. They had the best service and souvenirs our airline could offer.

The men pulled out cigars and settled in. They played cards, using our airline's monogrammed decks, and formed clouds of smelly smoke. While the passengers relaxed, I worked the rear galley and began organizing meal trays.

Once the services were completed, Gail and Nancy visited with the New Yorkers. I rearranged the galley compartments and cleaned the stainless steel counters. Everything was put away and I began to set up for the next meal.

Bobbi (far right) with fellow flight attendants

When Nancy came back, she reported that one of the gamblers said she was beautiful and offered her a mink coat "but only if he wins at poker."

"Did he ask for your telephone number?" I asked.

"No."

"Then how is he going to contact you? You'll never see him again."

I burst her bubble, but she didn't care and flirted with him anyway.

"He's old but cute," she added. "And I like his musky cologne."

All the passengers were in their forties and fifties, at least twenty years older than we were. The men teased and their wives glared. The few married men without their wives had removed their wedding bands. You could see the obvious white marks on their ring fingers.

Ginny, working in the front galley, responded to a passenger's call button. While she walked up the aisle, the group leader asked Ann Marie, the senior flight attendant, to join him behind the galley curtain.

Mr. Bianchi gave her a hundred dollars as a tip to share among the cabin crew. We rarely received tips; it was against our airline's policies. But temptation interfered. And twenty dollars each was a lot of money, one-third my monthly rent.

Mr. Bianchi told her to meet him at the hotel barbershop that evening. He wanted the flight attendants to be his guests for a dinner show.

After the flight, Gail, Nancy, Ginny, and I showered and dressed for dinner. Ann Marie met the group leader at the barbershop, located in the basement of the hotel. She noticed two intimidating men standing on each side of the doorway as she approached the shop.

"Mr. Bianchi paid his barber's bill from a briefcase filled with stacks of money," Ann Marie told us, her eyes wide with excitement. "This will be a great evening."

We gathered an hour later in the hotel lobby. All five flight attendants were dressed in their best and sexiest attire. I wore spiked heels, a string of pearls, and put on a simple black knee-length dress. From the front, I looked matronly. But in the back the dress was cut so low that it fell to my waist and I had to go braless.

Ginny was a blond who wore a teal mini-dress, showing off her long slender legs. Ann Marie had on a striped outfit, low cut in the front; Nancy let down her thick, brown hair; and Gail wore a dress of candy-apple red that emphasized her tiny waist. We looked fabulous.

Mr. Bianchi greeted us enthusiastically, kissing our cheeks. He flashed his diamond pinky ring and puffed out his chest as we accompanied him to the dinner show. A few of his friends joined the entourage and asked to be our escorts, offering their elbows for us to take.

Heads turned as we walked from the gold-embossed lobby to the show entrance, passing glittering chandeliers and regal columns. It seemed as if we were a parade of celebrities.

A special table for ten had been arranged at the center, right in front of the stage. The show began with beautiful women descending a wide staircase. They wore enormous headdresses with three-foot feathers protruding from them.

And they were topless. All the breasts one ever wanted to see were on full display. Abundant, high, and firm.

In the sixties, America was just beginning to over-come its prudish attitudes. As flight attendants, we seemed to be on the cusp of this change.

At midnight the men were still gambling. Nancy and Ann Marie joined them. Ginny, Gail, and I thanked Mr. Bianchi for a wonderful evening but declined to stay any longer. We were tired from working the flight and decided to go to our rooms.

"We're leaving tomorrow and have to get ready," Ginny said. "We're flying to Japan in the afternoon."

Before long, Nancy and Ann Marie gathered in our room and told us of their gambling bouts. Ann Marie won a few dollars, but Nancy lost her money. So did her escort. She wasn't going to receive a mink coat after all. We laughed at the outcome and encouraged her to start saving.

THE TET OFFENSIVE

Combat raged in Vietnam in the late 1960s, and I flew there as a flight attendant, bringing thousands of troops into the war zone. The communist North and the democratic South were engaged in an all-out civil war.

In January 1968, the North Vietnamese launched attacks below the demilitarized zone (DMZ), the border separating the two countries. This violent confrontation was called the Tet Offensive because it began during the lunar New Year or Tet holiday. As the South Vietnamese and their foreign counterparts observed a traditional cease-fire celebration, the North Vietnamese began their massive assault and moved south.

My airline transported soldiers into two airports that came under fire during the Tet Offensive. One was in Da Nang, a city that lies close to the DMZ, and the other was Tan Son Nhut Air Base, located near the city of Saigon. The attacks from the North continued for six months, and we, as crew members, endured the fright of rocket attacks and flying through flak.

The Viet Cong targeted major airfields and densely

populated South Vietnamese cities with an unprecedented barrage of rockets that threatened anyone nearby. As we came in for a landing in Da Nang one night, I looked out a nearby window and saw tracers coming at us. The chemically treated bullets looked like red ribbons painted in the black sky.

Once we touched down and taxied to the terminal, an officer boarded.

"Move it! Move it!" he yelled at the soldiers.

The airport was now under intense gunfire and the men raced from the plane. As sirens wailed, another guy in combat gear rushed up the stairs and entered our plane.

"That means you, too!" he ordered. "Move it! Get out of here!"

The crew bolted from the plane and rushed to a nearby bunker. We hunkered down as we crossed the tarmac, the flight attendants in skirts and high heels. All of us crouched in an underground shelter made of sand bags and waited for the detonations to stop.

In the darkness I squatted next to Robin and Connie. The ground shook as loud roars echoed across the night. The attack reached a blinding pitch as fireballs exploded nearby. My legs hurt from the awkward position of kneeling and leaning into a wall.

As I tried to stretch my legs, I heard another explosion rumble in the night, and I immediately gripped the hairy forearm of a nearby soldier.

We huddled together, wedged into the crypt-like cellar as the shelling continued. My heart pounded, my body shook, and the damp bunker smelled of body odors. Sweat poured from my body and soaked my underarms.

"God, please protect us." It was a mantra I repeated

over and over as I trembled with fear.

Finally we heard the all-clear signal. As I tried to stand, my knees buckled. With help in the darkness from unknown arms, I rose to my feet. We scrambled out of the bunker, escorted by helmeted soldiers, and returned to our plane.

The fuselage was peppered with bullet holes but the engines survived in good order. There were a few shrapnel marks that the engineer covered with speed tape, a material similar to duct tape. The maintenance men in Japan, our next destination, would repair any damage.

Connie looked at me and asked, "What happened to your leg?"

I looked down and saw blood streaming from a wound below my knee. My shredded stocking had fallen to my ankle, bunching around my mud-covered shoe.

"It must be from the bunker," I answered.

I cleaned my leg with materials from the jet's first aid kit and applied several bandages. With fresh stockings, l felt almost like new. Or so I thought. Between the hair-raising time in the bunker and the extra hour waiting for the shelling to stop, I was exhausted.

Luckily, we were able to ferry the plane to Yokota. Each flight attendant took a row of seats, lifted the arm-rests, and added pillows and blankets. We fell asleep within minutes. We were all emotionally drained.

Not all Vietnam flights were as dramatic. During six years of flying into the war zone, I had to run for cover only that one time. Soldiers in jeeps with rifles and machine guns constantly guarded us. When Tan Son Nhut became too dangerous, we flew into Bien Hoa, twenty miles away.

CAM RAHN BAY

Another Vietnam base was Cam Rahn Bay, an R&R (or rest and recuperation) destination for countless soldiers. The United Service Organizations sent many entertainers into the country during the war. The USO performers created all sorts of acts for the troops, lifting their spirits. We never knew what celebrity might be traveling with us to Vietnam.

On one occasion we had the Swedish actress Ann-Margret on board. She stood, as beautiful as ever, at the top of the portable stairs and did a little dance, wearing a mini-skirt and white boots. The troops surrounding our plane looked up in awe. Some dramatically collapsed on the tarmac. And from the bottom of the stairs they could see right up her skirt. Hoots and howls erupted.

Another time I had Roy Rogers, Dale Evans, and the Sons of the Pioneers, a group of singing cowboys that accompanied Roy and Dale on many of their professional engagements. The flight attendants asked them to sing "Happy Trails" and the crew and deploying soldiers joined in.

Sailors and Flight Attendants.

Later in the flight Dale became very quiet, absorbed in writing a book about the death of one of their adopted children. Roy stayed in the cockpit during most of the flight. All aspects of flying fascinated him and the crew loved having him there. They exchanged movie and flying stories, much to everyone's delight. I remember the huge gold ring that Roy wore. It was in the shape of a Western saddle and covered his ring finger from knuckle to knuckle. On the sides of the saddle were bright jewels: rubies, sapphires, and diamonds.

Most celebrities were kind and courteous. One, however, was not. He was short and arrogant. He had an aisle seat in the first row behind the galley wall. As the flight attendants walked past, he called us "darling" or "sweetie" and either tried to pull us onto his lap or slapped our backsides. Because he was such a military bigwig, we put up with his behavior. But no one liked it. Some of the men in his entourage seemed embarrassed and later apologized for his actions.

Throughout the Vietnam War the USO sent entertainers overseas, and we were privileged to escort them. On our way back to the States, the area by the rear galley often hosted impromptu jam sessions. The harmonious voices of entertainers, servicemen, and flight attendants filled the plane with pure passion, fueled by a love of country and the thrill of finally leaving Vietnam.

RUGBY AND ROMANCE

Nuns. That's what we called ourselves. Although some flight attendants had boyfriends at home, the others rarely dated while on the job. There was no way we could. We took military passengers to Vietnam, the cockpit men were too old, and our civilian passengers were traveling in groups, never to be seen again. Despite media rumors, romantic interests seldom blossomed while working on a charter flight.

The only sexual activity for nearly all flight attendants was with boyfriends at home. Even that could be a struggle. Most men did not understand the endless flight adjustments that occurred when their girlfriends worked for a nonscheduled airline.

Dates at base sites were constantly being tested. Several times as I dressed for dinner with Bob, the phone rang. The scheduling department informed me that I had to leave in a couple of hours. I'd be gone for two weeks.

Granted, the places we visited were beautiful and exotic. But if we ever did date on the flight line, it was almost always platonic. All that changed one day when our crew arrived in Hawaii.

"Finally, we're here," Dolly declared. "I can't wait to go swimming."

She leaned on the railing at the top of the portable stairs, lifting her face to the early morning sun. We had just worked a night flight from the Philippines, where we had had three days of rain. Dolly glanced beyond the terminal building toward the tropical mountains and mist-covered valleys. A cool breeze blew from the ocean.

"I need to work on my tan," I remarked, standing beside her. "Bob and I are going to a formal dance and my dress is sleeveless."

After clearing customs, the crew took a limo to the Ilikai, a luxurious hotel on Waikiki Beach. In the lobby we passed a group of rugby players. They were departing for an exhibition match as we were checking in. We stood in our tan and white uniforms at the reception desk and noticed the men staring at us.

The New Zealanders wore striped rugby jerseys and their muscles bulged under the cotton material. As one of the best teams in the world, the handsome boys were on an educational tour for both their country and the sport of rugby.

Later that afternoon, Jenny, Dolly, Jane, and I lay sunbathing on the beach. The eight-hour flight from Clark Air Force Base had exhausted us. All we wanted to do was lie on our towels atop the pearl-white sand and vegetate. We were so tired that we never even picked up our books.

A strapping young man approached us. "Hi. Didn't we see you in the lobby?"

Before long, four New Zealand men lay beside us. Normally we wouldn't have encouraged any conversation, talking only enough to be polite. But they were gorgeous.

Laughing and listening, we sat up. I wrapped my arms around my knees and looked out at the ocean as I listened to their New Zealand tales.

"I was raised on the South Island in Christchurch," Patrick said. "And I love to camp and fly fish."

He was not very tall, but quite muscular and with remarkably wide shoulders. Now a college student, Patrick supported himself with rugby scholarships. Ray, Mickey, and Al, all lanky athletes, came from the North Island. They also supported themselves with scholarships.

The eight of us body surfed, basked in the sun, and flirted. As the afternoon ended they invited us for dinner. We changed from bathing suits to dresses and met them on the tiled terrace located at the back of the hotel.

As we strolled along the beach to a Japanese restaurant, we began to pair up. Patrick and I walked side by side. Behind us were Dolly and Al. Following them were Jane and Mickey. Trailing quite a ways back were Jenny and Ray, both tall and dark haired. They looked like twins. We were all on tight budgets and agreed to go Dutch treat.

After their daily exhibition matches, they met us on the beach. We swam in the surf and then changed for dinner. The second night we walked the beach to a Hawaiian restaurant, barefoot with our dresses blowing in the wind. As I sat close to Pat, I noticed the smell of citrus fragrance on his neck. He held my hand under the table and occasionally squeezed my fingers.

On our return, the eight of us did all the free things within walking distance of the hotel. We wandered through a local park, window shopped along Ala Moana Boulevard, and visited nearby boat docks.

For our last night in Hawaii, the New Zealanders suggested we join them for pizza and beer in their hotel room. The next day they had to return to Auckland and we had to work a trip to California. They already had beer in their room and ordered pizza from the hotel.

Three of the men were staying in an Ilikai Hotel dorm room with a sliding glass door that opened to the ocean. They had three mini-dressers, three nightstands, and three single beds lined in a row, two feet apart. I thought of Goldilocks and the Three Bears.

Patrick bunked with two other rugby players in another room down the hall. The eight of us sat on the beds as if they were facing couches and talked of our futures. In her exuberant voice, Jane, a former Miss America contestant, added a few airline and modeling tales, spicy and funny.

We drank beer from cans and waited impatiently for the pizza. Dolly played her guitar and serenaded us with songs from *The Mamas and the Papas*. The sounds of the rolling waves and swaying palm leaves mingled with Dolly's sweet voice.

Smells of melting cheese and pepperoni arrived before the deliveryman. He handed us five pizzas and departed. In a matter of minutes the rugby players consumed one large pizza each. The last one was divided between Dolly, Jenny, Jane, and me.

"Wow! You guys can eat!" I exclaimed.

After finishing the pizza and drinking more beer, Ray dimmed the overhead light. We continued to talk while a soft breeze from the ocean swept into the room. With much laughter, the three couples collapsed on their parallel beds.

Standing in the corner, Pat wrapped his arms around me. I lifted my chin, and he lowered his lips to mine. In three days, that was our first kiss. I felt his heart beating against my body as he engulfed me in his arms. He bent down and kissed me again. My hands slowly rubbed his biceps.

"Let's get out of here," he said.

Pat and I walked out the patio doors and headed toward the beach. The moon rose over the horizon, its light rippling across the waves. He held my hand, and we stopped to kiss numerous times.

I wrapped the hem of my dress around my hips and walked into the warm ocean. Pat was right behind, laughing as he pushed me deeper into the surf. He pulled me back at the last moment to save me from a thorough soaking. Finally we ambled back to the hotel and took the elevator to my room. I flashed on memories of my father teaching me to drive and having The Talk.

At the door, Pat turned me around and gave me a passionate kiss. I didn't invite him into my room, but we hugged each other in a tight embrace.

"I'll send you letters," I said.

"Good-bye, my lovely," Pat said and he kissed me one last time. "I'll write when I get home."

When Jenny returned to our shared room, she told me, in her inebriated stupor, what had happened after I left.

"We did the unthinkable," she said, lowering her head. "We had sex."

All three couples in the same room, just two feet from each other. Talk about conduct unbecoming a flight attendant!

Early the next morning, while waiting for the soldiers to arrive at the airport, Dolly and I chatted about the girls' forbidden night of sin. They were shocked by their lack of discretion. None of them had ever had a sexual date while flying. We really were nuns—at least for the most part.

Two weeks later I received a letter from Pat. We wrote back and forth for almost a year. He told me of his Rugby adventures, and I wrote about my world travels. Eventually the letters slowed and finally stopped.

ICELANDIC INCIDENT

Transporting vacationers between Europe and the States was common. From London I had been assigned to work a ten-hour flight to the West Coast, with a refueling stop in Iceland.

The mechanical and fuel requirements involved more than an hour of ground time, and all passengers and flight attendants had to deplane. While inside the Keflavik terminal, the local cleaners straightened the airplane cabin and replenished supplies. The day was July 20, 1969.

Linda, Arlene, and I changed to high heels and put on our hats and coats. We followed the passengers into the small, rectangular terminal and inspected the local art.

"Why are there so many airmen?" Linda asked of no one in particular.

An airport employee overheard her and turned to answer the question.

"The U.S. built this airport during World War II," he said. "It was a refueling stop for American and Canadian warplanes."

Consequently, Keflavik, the only international airport in Iceland, was located in the center of an American military base. All passengers, even Icelanders, had to go through a United States checkpoint.

As we left the employee, I said, "Look at these photographs. They're amazing."

Lining the walls were framed pictures illustrating Icelandic volcanoes, fishing villages, and enormous ice flows. Standing in front of the photos, we commented about the austere lives of these Nordic people.

While Linda and Arlene continued to walk the length of the terminal, I wandered into a side office that looked like a classroom filled with tables and chairs. A group of airmen stared at a black and white television near the ceiling corner. The men seemed mesmerized.

I looked up and watched Neil Armstrong and Buzz Aldrin walk on the moon. My eyes stayed riveted to the screen as soldiers and passengers moved in and out of the room.

Armstrong had commanded the Apollo 11 spacecraft, accomplishing the most daring NASA expedition of the twentieth century. His famous words, "One small step for man, one giant leap for mankind," marked America's victory in the space race. I heard those historic words while staring at a small television in an Icelandic airport.

Transfixed, I watched the astronauts walk on the lunar surface and collect moon samples. They took photographs and performed several experiments. I never noticed anything else going on around me. It was as if I were hypnotized.

Finally, I turned around. The classroom was empty. I hurried back to the main building. Not a soul remained.

I raced to our airline's gate, but the door had been

locked. I looked out the large windows and saw my plane backing away.

Panic struck me. In high heels with my coat flapping, I ran the length of the narrow terminal.

"Let me out!" I screamed. "Help! I need help!"

A military man was sweeping one of the offices. He came out and asked, "What are you doing here? Your plane's already left."

"Tell them to stop," I begged.

He grabbed a telephone and called the tower.

"The pilot left one of his girls here. What should we do?" He said laughing as he spoke into the phone.

The tower notified the captain, and the taxiing plane turned back toward the terminal. Once the plane reached its stopping point, two airmen rolled the portable stairs into position. I dashed across the tarmac, up the staircase, and into the cabin.

When I burst through the entrance door, completely out of breath, the whole cabin broke into cheers and applause.

"Yeah! She's back!" one of the passengers shouted.

They thought my near miss was hysterical. The senior flight attendant, however, raged with fury.

"Where have you been?" Helen demanded, spitting the words as she spoke.

I told her about the television, the astronauts, and watching the moon landing. Behind the galley curtain, Helen continued to berate me.

"I'm furious. You really pissed me off. No crew member has ever, and I mean ever, been left behind. You are the first!"

By Federal aviation rules, a plane cannot take off

without a correct number of flight attendants per passenger. In case of an emergency, all flight attendants are needed to evacuate the passengers in the required ninety seconds. I knew I was going to be fired.

With luck, I escaped a negative report and possible termination. Because Helen had not counted the flight attendants, she would have had to share in the blame. Because the captain left the terminal without the proper number of flight attendants, he also was negligent. Consequently, nothing was reported.

Even so, the senior flight attendant and captain scrutinized my every deed for the rest of the flight. Later, Captain Carter took me aside and reprimanded me.

"God damn it!" he barked, glaring at me. "Do you know how much fuel and time we wasted because of you?"

Thank goodness this was the last leg of our two-week trip and we were heading home. I didn't have to work with either of them for many months.

Friendly crew members remembered my close call as another funny flight attendant incident. The moon landing was an historic event. But if I'd been left behind in Iceland, my airline career could also have been history.

SPANISH BULLFIGHT

In 1970 I decided to vacation in Spain. Using an airline pass, I flew Trans World Airlines from New York to Madrid. On the way I chatted with Brooklyn-based flight attendants, and we exchanged parallel narratives of unpredictable passengers and conflicts with crews.

For my initial night in Madrid, I stayed in a first-class hotel in the center of the city. The next morning I followed my usual custom of walking to the American Express office to meet other tourists and learn about nearby youth hostels. Wayne, Joanie, and Leigh, students from Pennsylvania, recommended an inexpensive inn not far from the historic area. That's where they were staying.

"It's simple but clean," Leigh said.

Back at my hotel, I checked out and took a taxi to the small pension. I placed my suitcase in a narrow, dorm-type room where cot-like beds filled the space. For three dollars a night each, five women had a single bed, a simple breakfast, and shared a communal bathroom. None of the women knew each other.

During the next few days, Joanie, Leigh, Wayne,

and I explored churches, museums, parks, and plazas. At the El Rastro, Madrid's ancient market, Joanie bought hand-decorated plates and I purchased an oil painting of Spanish laborers. It hangs in my kitchen today.

"Let's see a bull fight," suggested Wayne. "It's at the Plaza de Toros."

I had never been to one and agreed to join the group. We walked to the station and crammed ourselves into a jammed train car. The scent of sweat from the many squeezed travelers permeated the air. A few Spaniards tried to smoke, but they were so tightly packed they couldn't move their hands.

Wayne stood in front of me, but a man pushed between us. I held my purse close to my chest with both arms wrapped around it. The train careened from one side of the tracks to the other, and I grasped my wicker purse firmly to my body as I swayed with the masses.

When we approached the Plaza de Toros, the train jostled to a stop. Just as the doors slid open, a man standing behind me put his hand under my dress and pushed his fingers between my thighs.

"Cut it out!" I screamed, trying to turn my body away from him. But I was too tightly wedged between passengers and couldn't move. He kept his hand between my legs.

With a little relief from the shifting crowd, I released one hand from my purse and elbowed him as hard as I could. At the same moment the guy in front yanked my purse and jumped off the train. All the passengers crowded out at the same time, and the two men were lost in the horde.

Along with my money, I lost my airline tickets,

passport, American Express card, and immunization record. Not feeling safe to leave my valuables at the hostel with unknown roommates, I chose to take them with me. Now I had nothing.

Nevertheless, we continued with our plans to see a bullfight. Joanie and Leigh chose cheap seats, the ones located in the sun. Wayne and I climbed the bleachers and joined them. He had bought my ticket along with a meat-filled lunch roll and loaned me some money.

Trumpets began signaling the beginning of the spectacle. I looked around. Everyone wore bright clothes and wide hats. They quieted as the parade of matadors, their assistants, and horses marched into the sand-filled ring.

There were three matadors, all wearing sparkling outfits of sequins and gold thread, the *suit of lights*. As we learned, the event was for six bullfights, two per matador.

The trumpet sounded again, and two men with long lances rode blindfolded horses into the ring. The black bull charged, trying to topple the horses. The men thrust their lances into the attacking animal, weakening the bull's neck muscles. The horses originally did not have protective padding until an American woman protested their goring in the 1930s. The Spanish tradition changed, and horses today wear padded drapes.

The trumpet sounded yet again and two assistants entered. Their job was to place colorful sticks behind the bull's neck while the animal charged, helping the matador gauge the attack. Six barbed sticks protruded from the bull's withers.

With the bull's power diminished, the matador entered and began his passes with the red cape. He finally dealt a deathblow to the bull with a well-placed sword, high between the bull's shoulder blades.

One of the bulls refused to fight and jumped the fence into the outer ring, where the matadors, their assistants, and owners stood. As the bull raced around the outer ring, all the people jumped into the main ring. The workmen eventually got him back into the arena, but he still refused to fight and ran from everyone. Half a dozen cows entered the ring and the bull followed the females, exiting through another gate.

One of the matadors was terrible at performing the kill. It took him several attempts to insert the blade into the soft spot between the bull's shoulders and into the heart. The crowd booed him and he left in disgrace. After each fight mules dragged the dead bulls from the arena; a man followed, stooping to sweep the blood from the hard sand.

One of the matadors performed almost perfectly, and we heard cries of "Ole!" with every close pass of the bull to his body. In the end he received the bull's ear as a prize and loud cheers from the applauding audience.

After the sixth fight we left and boarded the train back to the city. We all agreed a bullfight should be seen once, to experience the culture of Spain.

The next day I went to Trans World Airlines and picked up duplicate tickets. That was easy. All I had to do now was retrieve my other documents. I took a bus to the American Embassy to obtain a replacement passport. They told me they had to wire New York to verify my records.

"Come back tomorrow," the receptionist said.

From the embassy I took another bus to the international health department to get my vaccinations. They refused to give me any shots without a passport. Once again I took a bus, this time to the American Express office. I needed a replacement credit card. They also refused my request. I had to have a passport.

The following day I returned by bus to the American Embassy.

"We haven't received a reply wire from New York," the clerk said. "We're still waiting. Come back tomorrow."

That evening I connected with Leigh, Joanie, and Wayne at one of Madrid's many bars. In Spain everyone enjoys at least a two-hour lunch and dinner starts after 9 p.m. We heard the song "Unchained Melody" by the *Righteous Brothers* as we entered the bar. American records were played throughout Madrid, and young locals loved to dance to rock and roll. And we loved to join them.

When we ordered beer and wine, the bartender gave complimentary finger foods—but only when we sat at the counter. With just one glass of wine, I enjoyed enough snacks to make my dinner. Sipping wine and tasting shrimp, we chatted about the day's activities and watched old men playing cards and smoking.

On my third trip to the American Embassy, I was once again told, "We have received nothing from New York. Come back tomorrow."

"What do you mean? I can't keep coming back. I need to get home! Let me speak to the ambassador," I demanded.

The clerk took me to a back office. I didn't meet with the ambassador, but I did sit down with an assistant. He asked numerous questions about my life, American history, and why I traveled to Spain. After I answered, he shook his head.

"I don't know what to do with you," he said. "Your accent and knowledge of the United States is good, but it does not qualify you as an American citizen. You could be Canadian."

He was adamant. He would not authorize a passport without proper identification. He required a response from the passport agency in New York.

Bending over with my hands covering my face, I broke into loud sobs.

"How will I ever get home?" I cried.

He came over and put his arm around my shoulders.

"We'll see what we can do," he said.

He walked out of the office and returned a few minutes later. He asked me to follow him to a room down the hall, where I had a photo taken. After an hour of film processing and information gathering, I received a United States passport.

Passport photo taken in Madrid

From there I went by bus to the health department and repeated my inoculations. Then I went back to the American Express office, received a duplicate credit card, and picked up some cash.

I gave the borrowed money back to Wayne and left the following day for San Francisco. My time in Spain cost twenty-six dollars. That money paid for all my food, drinks, transportation, and lodging. In spite of losing my purse, I had a fabulous vacation in Madrid. Four days later I returned to my airline duties, taking soldiers from Hawaii to the Philippines.

PHILIPPINE COCKFIGHT

Once we reached the Philippines, my flight attendant cohorts and I elected to venture away from Clark Air Force Base. Robin and Connie were California blonds and as adventuresome as I was. We had been invited to see a cockfight as guests of two army brothers, Jack and Craig Bingham. With crew cuts, white polo shirts, and tan slacks, they looked like typical, athletic Americans.

Get in, girls," Jack and Craig commanded, picking us up in a jeepney, a small taxi with open sides. Typical of Philippine vehicles, its windshield was framed in colorful balls of yarn and a large crucifix hung from the front mirror.

Cockfights are legal in the Philippines and are as popular as baseball is in the States. With a three-day layover we decided to sample the local sport.

On our drive through Angeles City, we passed numerous bars and strip joints. Brothels lined the streets, crammed between hair salons, clothing outlets, and souvenir shops. We saw thatched homes facing the narrow road, the small shacks built on four-foot stilts with pigs, chickens, and children running underneath. The youngest children scampered around wearing only T-shirts—no diapers and no pants. They played with coconut shells as they crawled in the dirt, imagining them to be racecars. A toddler hid behind his mother's skirt in an open doorway and stared at us as we waved a friendly *hello*.

We overtook a small horse pulling a wagon piled high with boxes. The driver whipped the thin animal and I saw open sores on its side. The harness chafed the bloody wounds and I wondered why the man didn't take better care of his injured animal.

Following an old battered truck, we choked from clouds of exhaust. The vehicle was piled with crates, holding dogs of all sizes and shapes.

"Where are they taking the dogs?" I asked.

"To market," Jack said.

"What do you mean?"

"Filipinos eat dogs," he added. "It's sad, so don't look."

Luckily, we turned off the main road and followed a line of cars along a short alley to our destination. Once we exited the jeepney, we could hear voices rumbling from inside a storage facility.

The five of us entered the dimly lit warehouse. It was crowded with men and smelled of stale tobacco and chicken manure. About fifty feet away we saw a raised platform surrounded by ropes. It looked like a miniature boxing ring. A spotlight shone on the canvas and lit up the elevated bleachers. Cocks were fighting, and no one noticed our arrival.

Seated nearest to the platform were the high rollers, hollering hundred-dollar bets as the cocks fought. The negotiations were fast and furious from all sides of the ring. Everyone seemed to be yelling.

As they shouted their bids, they stretched one hand toward the bid-taker while the other hand covered their mouths. In the Philippines, spitting, even accidentally, was considered offensive.

We noticed that long, razor-sharp knives or spurs had been taped to both of the bird's hind claws. The owners antagonized the birds by pushing them close together, then pulling them back. Over and over the birds were pushed and pulled, until their feathers flew. The cocks were now ready to fight.

Screeching and squawking, the colorful birds flew at each other with wings spread and their feet stretched out in front. Knives dug into the opposing bird's flesh. But there was no blood. Feathers absorbed the liquid and made the fight appear only slightly less obscene.

The owners were in the ring with their birds, encouraging and yelling. The referee stood near the action and judged the fight. Eventually one bird fell on his side, unable to stand, and the fight was called.

Jack and I climbed off the benches and walked to the dark section surrounding the arena. There were stacks upon stacks of birdcages. Under the glow of single light bulbs hanging from the rafters, owners attached spurs and cut off the cocks' red combs.

Specialists tended to wounds and bandaged birds that could be saved. The cocks that were not deemed worthy of saving were immediately killed. The owner took the bird's head in his hand and spun it around, snapping its neck. Then they chopped off their heads and hung them upside down, their blood dripping into a bucket. Another man plucked the dead birds and threw the carcasses into a wicker basket. They were destined to become someone's dinner later that evening.

Connie, Robin, and Craig joined Jack and me in the dark perimeter.

"Want to see a sex act?" Craig asked.

"What's that?"

"I'm not sure," he said. "Let's see."

SEXHIBITION

We were young, inquisitive, and thousands of miles away from home. All three of us grew up relatively sheltered and a sex act piqued our interest. What could be shoddier than the cockfight we had just seen? We followed the men into a small side room.

The five of us again sat on elevated benches about twenty feet from a central arena. Connie, Robin, and I looked prim and proper in our skirts and white blouses; the men looked like they were taking us on a date.

There were roughly thirty onlookers, but from the moment we arrived we were hit by the silence. Everyone stared at us, and no one made a sound.

A handsome man stepped onto the arena, wrapped in a terry-cloth robe. He sat on a folding chair, his side to the audience. In the center was a mattress-covered table.

In the background, soft music played. *Chances Are* by Johnnie Mathis came from a portable record player behind the stage. A stunning young woman entered wearing high heels, a white blouse, and a red skirt. She looked like a teacher.

Stopping in front of the young man, she slowly undid the buttons of her blouse. She paused, removed her bra, and turned to face us. Her breasts were high and firm, and she was exceptionally beautiful.

As the melody continued, she slipped off her skirt. Standing in only her stockings, a garter belt and high heels, she looked like the classic pin-up. She wore no panties, and we saw the fluff of her pubic hair.

The man in the robe beckoned her and she sat on his knees, gradually unrolling her stockings. After a few kisses, she arose and strolled to the table, sitting on its side and kicking off her shoes.

To the sounds of the song, she curled her body backwards and draped her thick hair over the edge of the mattress. We were close enough to see every detail.

Her hands cupped her breasts, pushing them upwards. Licking her fingers, she tweaked her nipples and moaned with pleasure. She gracefully placed her hands on her thighs and gently pushed her fingers into her vagina.

The young man approached the bed and leisurely dropped the robe. He was huge and completely erect. Robin, Connie, and I gasped in unison.

He started rubbing her feet and spread her legs as he climbed on the table, running his tongue between her thighs and up toward her torso. When he was completely on top of her, he kissed and lightly blew on her nipples. He positioned his penis to her vagina and slowly entered.

I glanced at Connie, sitting with her back straight, her hands folded in her lap. Instead of being at a sex exhibition, she could have been in church. Robin leaned forward, her fingers gripping the edge of the bench. She looked like she was attending a football game. I sat still and thought of my father's anxiety about my chosen profession.

We heard the pounding of their thrusts. Then the climax. But not another sound. Dead silence.

They lay together for a moment, exhausted and spent. A glow of sweat engulfed their bodies. A maid came in with towels and robes, wrapping them as they dismounted the bed. Despite the romantic music, the scene was too vivid and the lights too bright.

"Most of the time, I'm told, you hear whistles and catcalls," Jack whispered. He added, "I think the soldiers were embarrassed to have women in the room."

Another event started soon after—one between a donkey and a woman. The five of us decided we had had enough local "entertainment." Even my free-spirited mother would have been horrified.

Our ride home was unusually quiet. We had been overwhelmed by the drama, and our hollow reactions made our escorts uncomfortable. At the cinderblock motel we left the jeepney and walked to our rooms.

"Do you think the other gals will believe us?" I asked.

CHILDBIRTH OVER
THE PACIFIC

Our flight from the Philippines to Hawaii started out as routine as ever—military men and their families returning to the United States. We stood at the top and bottom of the portable stairs, wearing white gloves as we welcomed the passengers. The plane wasn't full, and the laughing soldiers spread themselves throughout the cabin. After we completed the emergency demonstration, we checked that all passengers had buckled their seat belts.

Once the jet leveled off, Jean and I changed into our aprons and passed out blankets, pillows, and magazines to those passengers in the rear of the plane. Meanwhile, Linda set up the stainless steel counter across the front of the galley. She started brewing coffee and arranged the trays and rolls for the dinner service.

The flight to Honolulu was smooth. The sunny skies belied what was to come. After serving dinner and picking up dirty trays, we completed a coffee service and sat down to eat our own meals. Night had now overtaken the plane. As we flew east, most of the passengers fell asleep. A few were reading, their tiny lights dotting the dark cabin interior.

Before starting a breakfast service, Jean and I checked those passengers who might have wanted some extra coffee or juice. We verified bathroom supplies and wiped off the counters, mirrors, and sinks. One lavatory was occupied.

"I'll check it later," I said.

After a half hour, the lavatory was still locked. Jean stood beside me as I knocked on the door.

"Is anyone in there? Do you need help?"

No one answered.

Using my fingernail, I pushed the lock mechanism to the right and released the door. Not wanting to embarrass anyone, we cautiously peeked in.

There on the toilet seat sat a young Filipino girl in a flowered dress. She was folded over at the waist, her head resting between her knees. Her hands and dark hair dropped to the floor in front of her. She looked dead.

"Are you all right?" I asked. No answer. She wasn't dead, but she was definitely unconscious.

Jean telephoned Margie, the senior flight attendant, and informed her of the situation. Margie notified the captain.

"Linda, we have an emergency. Will you make up a bed?" I asked.

She told the passengers in the last two rows about the urgent situation and asked them to find other spots to sit. She then pulled up the three armrests on the last row and pushed forward the seatbacks in the second to the last row. Linda placed blankets and pillows on the three seats and formed a simple makeshift bed.

"Let's grab her under the arms," I suggested.

Jean and I half carried and half dragged the young woman from the lavatory. After we rested her body in the newly created bed, we lifted her feet.

A request was made over the PA system: "Ladies and gentlemen, is there a doctor on board?"

An abrupt hush enveloped the plane. Passengers glanced around, attempting to see what was happening. Although we had no doctor on board, we did have a medic. Tom Delaney stood up and walked toward the front. He was tall and thin with brown hair, wearing a khaki uniform.

"I'm a medic. Can I help?"

Margie related the facts about the unconscious teenager and they both walked to the rear of the plane. While Tom examined the passed out girl, Jean and I taped a blanket to the overhead bins to give them privacy.

Tom turned to us and asked, "Where's the baby?"

Confused, we looked at each other.

"What baby?" we said in unison.

"She just gave birth. Where's the baby?"

"We found her unconscious in the bathroom," Jean answered.

Although the young woman was now awake, she did not speak English and we were unsure of her medical situation.

Tom went into the lavatory she had been using. He reached below the toilet bowl into the waste container, and swished his arm around. He brought out a dead baby.

Although covered with brown slime, it was perfectly formed except for a large black bulge on the back of his head. It had been submerged in the toilet for almost an hour.

Tom placed the baby boy in the sink and turned to explain the catastrophe.

"It didn't make full term," he said. "It was probably in the womb only five months."

He and I stood crowded in the small confines of the bathroom, gazing at the tiny infant. It smelled like human waste. I had never seen a newborn before and bent down to inspect it.

"Look," I said, pointing to the back of its head. "There's a bruise."

"It could be a deformity," Tom said. "That might have caused the mother to abort. Or the bruise might have happened when the baby fell into the toilet."

He wrapped the baby in a garbage bag (the only large, clean item we had on the plane) and placed it on the lavatory floor. I locked the door and returned to the young woman, who was now sobbing on the makeshift bed. I felt her damp skin and wiped her forehead.

From her hand signals I understood she was thirsty and gave her a cup of water. I propped her up with pillows, permitting her to easily drink.

Tom rubbed her belly, and eventually the birth waste was eliminated. Again he wrapped it in a garbage bag and I placed it in the restroom. Tom returned to his seat once he was sure we could handle the situation.

"Thanks, Tom," Jean and I said, our words flowing together.

Margie came to the aft galley and said, "An ambulance will be waiting when we arrive in Honolulu."

Linda sat with the girl, stroking her arm and talking softly to her. Jean and I rested on the rear jump seats, exhausted from the traumatic experience. Before long a young sailor appeared. He wore his Navy uniform and had a blond buzz cut.

"Have you seen my wife?" he asked. "I fell asleep and can't find her."

Jerry Smith, an eighteen-year-old from Pittsburgh, had married a Filipino teenager a few months earlier. His wife Divina didn't know many English words, but Jerry said they loved each other. They were planning to have a family and start a new life together in America.

We told Jerry about Divina's loss of the baby and brought him to her side. He sat on one of the folded seats in front of the makeshift bed and held her hand, talking tenderly with her.

After the breakfast service we cleaned the galley and prepared for landing. Jerry and Divina sat up, and I placed a pillow between the seat belt and Davina's stomach.

An ambulance drove up after the plane taxied to the terminal. Two medics in white uniforms boarded the rear of the plane and placed the two evidence bags into a container.

"We'll take her to immigrations first and then right to the hospital," one said. "Don't worry. She won't have to get out of the ambulance."

They placed Divina on a stretcher and began to remove her from the aft seats. She reached out for Jerry, crying hysterically. She wanted him to come with her, but the Navy wouldn't allow him to deplane. He had to continue flying to Travis Air Force Base in California.

Both of them wept and she grabbed his shirt, trying to keep him with her. We watched the sad drama unfold as the medics took her down the stairs. They put her in the ambulance, closed the door, and raced away from the plane. Jerry bent his head and wiped his face.

"I can't believe we lost our baby," he moaned.

Linda, Jean, and I listened to his heartbreaking words. Maybe something good would come from their sad beginnings. We hoped there would be a happy ending when they eventually connected in the States.

VIETNAM TURNAROUND

Our airline flew to Vietnam several times a week. I was scheduled to work these flights at least once a month. We called the route, the "Vietnam turnaround." Five hours from Japan, minimal ground time in Vietnam, and five hours back.

Our plane flew through flak many times when we came in to land. At night you could see the tracer rounds, bullets treated with chemicals. They looked like fireflies or red flares coming at the plane. Being young and naïve, I never realized these were live rounds aimed at our jet. Some of the young soldiers were scared. One cried and wrapped his arms around his body as he looked out the plane's window.

It was always an adventure, and I never knew when to expect an unsettling shock.

The Boeing 707 jet was one of the largest passenger airplanes in the 1960s. Flying into Saigon during the war years meant landing at the busiest airport in the world. Helicopters, DC-3s, DC-6s, DC-8s, 707s, fighter jets, and small, single-engine planes were all landing and taking off at the same time. It was a traffic jam. The control tower employees had their hands full and were often overloaded.

On one particular flight we were beginning our final approach into the Saigon airport. I was still in the aisle, finishing last minute checks of seatbelts and tray tables.

All of a sudden a small aircraft passed beside us, going in the opposite direction. Our wings seemed to literally overlap. We came within inches of a mid-air crash.

The moment our plane stopped at the terminal, Captain Carter rushed from the cockpit. I had never seen him so infuriated. His face was bright red.

"Get out of my way," he shouted, shoving his way past the ground crew. He ran into the control tower, confronting the first employee he saw.

"Why did you allow a takeoff while we were landing?" he demanded. "Damn it! We were both using the same runway!"

"It's not my job to tell you of private planes," the young employee responded. "I only report on military flights."

Captain Carter grabbed the man by his shirt and raised him a foot off the ground.

"Goddamn it! We almost crashed!"

He threw the employee back into his chair and roared at the surrounding men, "You radio us about every plane—no matter what!" And with that, he stormed out of the building.

He was still red-faced when he returned to our aircraft. The soldiers had already left and the cleaning crew had now boarded the jet. We followed Captain Carter to the airport cafeteria and listened to his retelling of the tower incident.   He sputtered with fury as he recounted the confrontation.

While sitting at the table with the captain, the waiter cautioned us not to have ice in our sodas. "Gooks are putting glass slivers in the ice," he said, as he wiped his hands on his white apron.

We reflected on this latest threat, the need to stay vigilant, and thought how lucky we'd be to leave Saigon.

Thirty minutes later the flight deck crew completed a walk-around, inspecting the fuselage for anything odd before entering the cockpit. This was a normal procedure at every refueling stop, whether in Vietnam or stateside. As I mentioned earlier, they often saw shrapnel or bullet holes and covered them with speed tape until they could be repaired in Japan.

While the cockpit men were performing their duties, Patty and I walked outside and encountered two garbage ladies looking in trashcans. They wore *ao dai* outfits: long, tight-fitting tunics in pastel colors over pajama-like pants. The paneled dress had a high collar, was buttoned down the front, and had slits to the waist on both sides.

In the distance we noticed a young woman with long black hair picking through another trashcan. She was exceptionally beautiful and caught our eye. The woman sorted through the leftovers and trash thrown out by the restaurant, to use either for herself or for bartering.

Surprisingly, this was a fairly decent job. It provided them with a little income during a time when jobs in Vietnam were practically nonexistent. It was also a relatively safe occupation.

Flight attendants with Vietnamese women

Leaning on a jeep with Patty inside

Once the soldiers had assembled, Captain Carter called us back to duty. Patty and I walked to our assigned positions and greeted the men.

"Welcome back, soldier," I said, standing at the bottom of the ramp.

The homebound G.I.s climbed the portable stairs and entered the cabin. We smiled at them and thanked them for their service.

I looked over their heads and noticed olive duffle bags going up the escalating ramp into the cargo area. I also saw a large cluster of black body bags ready to be loaded into a nearby Army plane. The fate of these other warriors made it hard for me to stay focused on the ones climbing the portable stairs, the happy men now returning home.

During all flights from Vietnam, we had to be very careful when waking soldiers. Because they were combat veterans, they sometimes exploded upward, throwing punches. We knew to stand behind their seats and touch their shoulders lightly, staying out of harm's way.

During this particular leg of the trip, two episodes caused me to ponder the fate of these returning veterans. We were a few hours into the flight when I visited with a couple of soldiers who were standing in the aisle, smoking and laughing. I asked about their opinions of the Vietnamese.

One reached into his pocket.

"This is how we left Charlie," he said, using a slang word for the Viet Cong.

He brought out a tan-colored finger wrapped in white tissue. I gagged in disgust.

"That's awful," I said and turned my back, walking

to the rear galley.

If he had been expecting praise, he certainly didn't receive it from me. Although I was proud of this young man's service, I disliked the trophy exhibit. Perhaps my negative reaction made him cautious about displaying severed body parts in the future.

On our flight to Yokota Air Base I worked the rear galley, organizing a meal and two beverage services. As I squatted in the galley, my knees almost touching the floor, I pulled breakfast trays from bottom containers and changed them to higher locations, making it easier and faster to serve.

While I was in this awkward position, I heard a loud slapping sound. Looking up, I saw a soldier above me. He glared at me, staring straight into my eyes, and smashed a clenched fist into his open palm.

He kept slamming his fist harder and faster, again and again. His fierce stance and angry look frightened the hell out of me.

I hesitated, not knowing whether I should stand or stay squatting. My heart pounded loud enough for me to hear. I remained scrunched with my body close to the floor. In a minute or so two military policemen came up and surrounded the soldier.

"Let's go back to our seat, Jay," one said as he hand-cuffed him.

The MP turned him around and walked Jay toward the front of the cabin. I stood and took a deep breath.

"What's that about?" I asked the other MP.

"He has some drug issues. We're taking him back to a Texas hospital. Jay needs to recuperate before we can tell his parents he's back in the States."

"Why was he loose? He scared me to death."

"We thought he'd be fine just going to the bathroom. He couldn't escape."

"No, but he could have killed me."

"Don't worry. We'll keep him secure from now on."

The MP returned to his seat, and I was once again left to ponder the tragedies of war. How sad for Jay and his family. I took a moment to collect myself as I sat in the rear jump seat, praying that he would recover. Even today, I still think of him occasionally.

COCKPIT FIASCO

"Who wants coffee?" I asked.

The seatbelt sign had been turned off and, as the senior flight attendant, I served the flight crew. I removed my uniform jacket, donned my apron, entered the cockpit, and took beverage orders before lunch. Three asked for coffee and one wanted tea.

Because of FAA regulations, I delivered meals to the two pilots (captain and first officer) thirty minutes apart. In case one of them became sick from a tainted dinner, the other could still command the aircraft. I asked the captain, "Do you want to eat first?"

While I was chatting, I noticed a slight smell of alcohol coming from the engineer, John Cramer. He was short and balding, and squirmed when he talked. He sat behind the first officer facing the illuminated engineer's panel. All four cockpit crew members—captain, first officer, engineer, and navigator—were retired military, twenty to thirty years older than the flight attendants.

"I have a story to tell you," John said.

My rapport with the flight crew was considerate and professional. I willingly stayed to hear his story.

When John stood, the foul smell of alcohol hit me. I ignored the odor and kept a pleasant smile on my face, trying to be sympathetic.

The story turned out to be a joke, and when John came to the end he had a wicked sneer on his face. For the dramatic punch line, he placed his hands on my breasts and rotated his fingers as if he were turning dials.

I was stunned. Frozen in place, I didn't know how to respond. A slight snicker broke the dead silence. The sound interrupted my spell; and I stomped out, slamming the door behind me.

I allowed no flight attendants to enter the flight deck. The cockpit crew members were left to their own devices. If they wanted drinks or meals they had to exit the cockpit, walk to the galley, and wait on themselves.

Usually they had periodic visits from the flight attendants. We would have delivered food, coffee, and much appreciated conversation. But for the next six hours they received not a speck of attention. The hours in the cockpit must have gone by at a snail's pace.

Captain Morris never requested that I resume a cockpit service. Had he done so I would have had to comply, as captains have unconditional authority on planes, but he never did. The cockpit men moved around us as we continued to work the galleys and cabin. We ignored them completely.

I could have been fired for my retaliation, but nothing was reported. They knew they were in the wrong—not only for the highly inappropriate joke, but because the engineer was allowed to violate the 24-hour liquor curfew required by our airline.

We landed that evening at Travis Air Force Base. The hour-long ride to Oakland was unusually quiet, devoid of chatter or laughter. No one said a word, and the only sound was the engineer snoring as we drove in the darkness to headquarters.

When we arrived at the control center, Captain Morris took me aside and apologized.

"It won't happen again."

That was the last time I saw John Cramer. I don't know if he was fired or if he quit. Either way, it was good riddance to him and his unprofessional behavior.

BRACE FOR LANDING!

"This is great, Robin," I said. "I love it when we ferry the plane."

"I agree. Getting paid to sleep is the best way to work."

A flight without passengers was a prized luxury. We lifted armrests and made beds out of seat rows. After throwing pillows and blankets on the makeshift bed and buckling ourselves in, we were sound asleep within minutes after takeoff.

It was January, and we were flying five hours across a wintry landscape, from Oakland to McGuire Air Force Base in New Jersey. I was the senior flight attendant on this particular flight. Once we picked up our scheduled MAC (Military Airlift Command) soldiers, we would continue flying to Frankfurt, Germany.

Captain Chapman, our pilot, was a favorite of the flight attendants. He was known to be charming and professional, with a great sense of humor. When we arrived at McGuire, snow was falling with tremendous intensity.

The massive snowstorm battered the entire East Coast. Air Traffic Control had diverted all other aircraft. Wind whipped around our plane as it descended, and we braced ourselves against the raging crosswinds.

I struggled into the cockpit, grabbing the door-frame, and listened to the captain's instructions.

"Just in case we can't land," Captain Chapman yelled, "tell the girls to be ready for a go-around."

I watched the blizzard blur the runway lights in the distance. The deafening sound of pelting hail and wind made hearing almost impossible.

With no passengers, the flight attendants seated themselves throughout the jet. Just as we touched down a ferocious crosswind hit us and we flew sideways. A powerful thrust from the engines forced us back into our seats and the aircraft started climbing. The plane lurched again and we began circling.

Once again we approached the runway. I entered the cockpit to check on our status. Captain Chapman turned his back to me, taking control of the yoke, and prepared for another approach.

The engineer told me, "The weather's fluctuating between minimums. They've cleared us for Philly...just in case we need to divert."

I left the cockpit and latched its door open. Secured in an aisle seat in the first row, I watched the captain fight to keep the jet aligned in the powerful crosswinds and blinding snow.

One wing dropped and seemed to scrape the tarmac. Captain Chapman pulled back on the control column and turned the yoke, leveling the plane.

The second approach had failed just like the first.

Captain Chapman ran his hand through his graying hair.

"We'll make one last try," he told me. "If we can't land, we'll fly to Philadelphia."

I informed the flight attendants and said, "Let's move to the rear."

Gripping the backs of the seat cushions, the five of us stumbled to the last aisle seats on the plane.

"Get in the brace position," I ordered.

With fear racing through our bodies, we grabbed our ankles and put ours heads between our knees. I pulled my seat belt as tight as possible and prayed.

Glancing at us in the brace position, the engineer commented, "Now that's what I call a vote of confidence."

On the third try we landed at the McGuire base. The jet whipped along the runway, lurching with every crosswind.

Once we stopped, Robin called out, "Wow! That's a flight I'll never forget."

Being a girl from sunny California, her comment rang true. It certainly did for me, and I grew up in snowy Connecticut.

After we gathered our belongings and the flight attendants changed into boots, we trudged toward the terminal, bent into the storm, the wind and snow slapping at our faces. I was freezing.

Once inside the building, we brushed our coats and headed for the coffee counter. The cockpit crew removed their outerwear and uniform jackets. The captain's and first officer's shirts were wringing wet. I cradled a cup of tea and listened to Captain Chapman recite the mantra of flight crews: "Hours of boredom punctuated by moments of sheer terror."

G.I.'S ON A RAMPAGE

"What a great time we had this week, the waves are really picking up," I said, greeting the flight crew that had just arrived from Travis. We were in Hawaii, and our crew would continue on the outbound flight to the Philippines.

Judy, the senior flight attendant for the arriving crew, slammed some papers in my hands and stormed past me. She followed the other crew members into the terminal, never stopping to chat.

"What's going on?" I asked.

Judy was usually so nice. Why was she in such a rush to get inside? I stood in the Hawaiian sun at the bottom of the boarding ramp, looking at her papers. Then I understood why she was in such a bad mood.

Judy reported that no officer had been on the military flight from California. As a result, the drafted soldiers were drunk, rowdy and abusive. I had read negative reports about crew members, but I had never read one about unruly passengers. Had the flight really been that awful?

When our crew boarded the plane, it looked like a

bomb had exploded inside. Papers, blankets, pillows, and food were thrown all about the cabin.

Captain Myers, a retired flight instructor, glanced at the mess as he stepped into the cockpit.

"Wow. The cleaning guys aren't going to be happy."

Well, neither was the cabin crew. As senior, I had to organize the other flight attendants and help them do their jobs, while avoiding the mess throughout the cabin. It took the cleaning crew an extra hour to make the plane presentable. While we were checking and cleaning, the soldiers were inside the terminal, possibly still drinking.

Once we were notified of a departure time, the flight attendants went to their assigned positions and welcomed the men as they climbed the ramp stairs. They had been on the plane five hours from California and had another eight hours to fly to the Philippines. Then they had three more hours to Vietnam.

I noted that they were laughing and poking each other as they boarded. The smell of alcohol saturated their clothes. It seemed like they were going to a party, not to war.

"Hey Jimmy, look at the fresh meat," one said, jerking his thumb at me as he went past.

We toured the cabin interior and checked their seatbelts, seat backs, and tray tables. I approached a soldier in an aisle seat with a blanket in his lap.

"Is your seat belt fastened?" I asked.

"Why don't you check?" he said and grabbed my hand, shoving it into his crotch.

All the nearby men laughed. The whistles and jeers began. We had barely left the terminal, and I knew this would be an unforgettable trip.

As we taxied to the runway, I entered the cockpit and told the captain what had transpired.

"Not to worry. They'll fall asleep as soon as we're airborne."

He announced over the PA system, "I want you fellows to respect the flight attendants."

His wimpy message was greeted by more catcalls. We could hear the whistles in the cockpit even with the door tightly closed.

I left the flight deck and plunked down on the forward jump seat next to Connie. Once we were airborne, I mentioned the seat belt incident.

"The same thing happened to me!" Connie exclaimed.

We braced ourselves for what was to come, but we truly had no idea.

After we were airborne and the no-smoking sign had been turned off, we walked through the cabin taking beverage orders. As Susan left the aft galley, someone grabbed her ankle and smacked her rear end. Robin saw a man expose and stroke his penis before she fled to the rear of the plane. I had pillows and blankets thrown at me. One pillow was soaked with sticky semen. Every flight attendant was harassed and grabbed.

I charged into the cockpit. "What should we do now?" I demanded.

Captain Myers suggested having all five flight attendants enter the cockpit.

"If I lower the cabin's oxygen level, the soldiers will pass out," he said.

After some discussion among the flight crew, he reconsidered.

"Damn. It's just my luck that one of those bastards would sue me."

Since I was the ranking flight attendant, the captain asked me to stay in the cockpit. "The others should lock themselves in the restrooms."

By phone I notified the flight attendants of the captain's instructions. Captain Myers kept the seatbelt sign illuminated and turned off all cabin lights except for the emergency floor panels. By doing so, he hoped the soldiers would eventually fall asleep.

I sat crowded in the cockpit on the narrow jump seat. When I cracked the door open and peered out, a major free-for-all ensued. Military chants and filthy sex songs resonated throughout the plane. They had stimulated themselves into an unbelievable frenzy.

After a few more hellish hours the men quieted, but the flight attendants remained locked in the restrooms. While sequestered, they read magazines and awkwardly napped, their heads resting on pillows atop the chrome counters. Only one lavatory remained open.

During the entire eight-hour flight we presented no meals and no beverages. I looked at my watch to see how much time we had before landing. An hour before we approached the Philippines, we exited the lavatories and took our assigned places. Finally, the jet landed.

The soldiers silently deplaned, not quite the boisterous group of G.I.'s that we had picked up in Hawaii. I handed my report papers to the incoming senior flight attendant and wished her luck.

She looked incredulously at my write-up and said, "Really?"

"You wouldn't believe it!"

On all three legs of that flight from the West Coast to Vietnam, the passengers received negative reports. It was the first time such a thing had happened. From then on, no military men were allowed to travel as a group without a certain number of officers on board.

"Our flight made military airline history," Captain Myers stated on our return trip to California.

He almost seemed proud of the accomplishment. Not so for us, the ones working the cabin in all that chaos.

ADVENTUROUS PHILIPPINE JOURNEY

The Philippine town of Angeles City surrounded Clark Air Force Base and provided an assortment of business activities: handmade wares, beauty salons, clothes made specifically to our measurements, and prostitution.

During Clark layovers, the flight attendants stayed in a white cinderblock motel encircling a welcoming swimming pool. It was the best place in town. Three meals a day came to less than five dollars and our per diem allowance was twenty-five dollars. We always made extra pay while at Clark, but ended up spending most of it on clothes and gifts.

When we wanted to buy certain outfits, we went to Rosa's, a seamstress who catered to flight crews and the military. We would show her pictures of a certain dress, have our measurements taken, and pick out the material. The outfit was often completed before our next flight.

At the local spa, we had haircuts and styling, nail manicures, and facials. And we had body massages. After standing in high heels for many hours, I loved to have my feet rubbed. The hard kneading almost bruised my heels and inner soles, but it felt wonderful.

Wearing a formal dress that had been made in the Philippines. Maroon velvet skirt with crystals and sequins on top.

The first time I experienced a massage, I lay nude on a cotton-draped table. A small cloth covered my torso. As the young masseuse rubbed my body, she touched me high between my thighs, stroking in places I had never explored myself. I sat straight up on the table, bright red with embarrassment.

"Stop!" I shouted.

Throwing her black hair over her shoulder, she and the other girls giggled at the awkwardness I felt. They were comfortable with their bodies and didn't mind touching parts of other women's bodies. From then on, I limited massages to my back, arms, and feet.

At the local market we bought hand-woven baskets, monkey pod bowls, and shell placemats. The soldiers liked the paintings on black velvet, Elvis and Christ being the most popular.

On one flight to the Philippines we had an unexpected layover of one week. Mandy and I decided to visit Baguio, a city in the mountains, eighty-five miles from the base.

It never occurred to us to ask permission. We left our metal suitcases in the room and took off with just our small in-flight bags.

Leaving the designated lodging was against airline rules. When at a layover station, we were "on call" at all times. If we were going to be away from the assigned hotel for more than four hours, we were to notify the captain. This was the time before cell phones. Telephone calls in foreign countries were irregular and not dependable. We were taking a huge risk.

Mandy and I caught a jeepney from the base to the Angeles City station where we boarded a bus heading to Baguio. People, animals, and packages filled the vehicle. There were even men on top, holding onto ropes that wrapped the crates and luggage.

I sat on an aisle seat beside an older woman. She wore a bright yellow dress with puffy sleeves and held half a dozen parcels on her lap. Mandy sat in front of me, next to a young mother with two babies, an infant and a toddler.

There were live chickens contained in empty feed sacks piled in overhead racks. Pink piglets squealed in tiny crates and packages were everywhere.

We sat on slatted wooden benches and kept the windows open for fresh air. The woman next to Mandy bared her breasts and fed both children as we climbed steep, twisting mountainsides to the Camp John Hay Airbase.

We took hairpin turns with no guardrails and crossed narrow bridges. When we came to a stream, everyone exited the vehicle and waded across while the bus was driven to the other side. Then we took our seats again.

We passed numerous flooded fields and saw the ever-present farmer, wearing a cloth skirt and working his water buffalo. They toiled as a team to cut furrows through the rice fields. The sinewy farmer draped the rope harness around his shoulders as he guided the primitive plow through the mud. For thousands of years farmers have used these same methods to work the mountain terraces.

Finally, after three hours, we arrived at the 5,000-foot Hay Airbase. It was resort-like, with a beautiful golf course, an elegant hotel, and charming cabins. The air was clean and cool and smelled of pine trees.

As we stepped from the bus, I noticed my body hurt from the long, bouncing ride. The slats of the wooden seats left red horizontal marks on my back and cut notches into the flesh along my spine.

Once our overnight luggage was placed in a stone cottage, we left to shop the local market, famous for carvings created from monkey pod wood. We perused the many tent-covered stalls and bargained with local merchants. I bought a three-foot carving of a water buffalo for twenty-five pesos, or a little more than six dollars, and had it delivered to my cabin.

At another open booth we met some Negritos—

small, dark men with tightly curled black hair. They looked similar to African pygmies and were known as tough Filipino warriors.

"This is the way we kill birds and small game," one of the Negritos said.

He demonstrated his hunting techniques by hitting a target twenty-five feet away with darts from a blowgun.

On our return to the hotel we passed a water buffalo tied to a tree. Two men in loincloths stood by it. As we wondered what they were up to, the scene before us suddenly shifted.

With a slash of his knife, one man severed the buffalo's throat artery. There was no noise; the buffalo just stood, dazed, with blood gushing from his neck. Then he collapsed to his knees and the men pushed him over on his side. Before he had even stopped breathing they started hacking into his stomach, removing the innards, and slicing off the hide.

With a nudge from Mandy, we continued to our cottage. As there were no locks on the door, some employees had entered to bring us hot tea. A blaze from the fireplace warmed the room and my monkey pod carving sat in the corner. We freshened up and walked to the celebrated restaurant, located inside the hotel.

While waiting for a table, two wealthy Filipinos asked if we would like to join them. We sat at a white-clothed table with Fermin and Rosito, business contractors with the U.S. military. They were married men and just wanted company. Fermin wore a shiny silk suit and Rosito had on a cashmere blazer. They both wore turtleneck shirts underneath their jackets.

As soon as the waiter came, they each ordered balut,

an Asian delicacy. Fermin wanted us to sample the unique dish. Mandy and I ordered a simpler fare and talked with them about local customs.

When the balut arrived, I almost choked. In Fermin's steaming bowl a tiny duck embryo floated, cooked just before hatching from the egg. You could clearly see the shape of the duck fetus, its little wings, feet, and beak. Rosito's duck arrived still in its shell.

Rosito pierced his warm egg and sucked the juice. Next he peeled off the top third of the shell and showed us the tiny duck inside, already coated with feathers. He added salt to the balut and took a bite. I could hear the crunching of the bones. More salt, another bite. We weren't about to share in this delicacy. In fact, we didn't stay for dessert but excused ourselves and returned to our cottage.

Canoeing in the Philippine mountains.
Mandy sits in back; I'm in front.

The next day Mandy and I hired local fisherman to take us canoeing. We wore sleeveless dresses, as slacks were rarely worn away from home. They paddled us in dugout canoes through a thick jungle forest. We passed small villages surrounded by towering palm trees, where native women went about their daily duties: cooking over fire pits, washing clothes in the river, and hanging them on bushes to dry. On our way back to Hay Camp, we listened to the chatter of monkeys and saw colorful birds high in the trees.

Mandy and I decided to go first class and take an Air Force bus back to Clark. It had padded seats and air conditioning. My buffalo carving sat in one of the blue plastic seats, secured by some scarf material I had purchased at the market. Forty-five years later, I still have the carving. Many children have ridden it throughout the years, and at Christmas time it sports a red satin bow.

When Mandy and I arrived at the base hotel, no one had missed us. We told stories of our Baguio journey while enjoying our last day of sunbathing. We lay on chaise lounges around the swimming pool and heard tales of the other flight attendants' adventures. The next day we returned to work and flew a planeload of soldiers to Hawaii for a week of R&R.

JAPANESE AUTUMN

Once when I worked a flight to Tokyo in late November, our airline placed the crew in a small inn next to an elevated railroad track. As a senior flight attendant, I had the room to myself. Besides listening to the noise of passing trains, I became mesmerized by the flashing neon lights outside my window. It was cold with snow on the ground, and my room had no heat.

Without a telephone and too tired to walk to the front desk, I decided to stay put. After twenty hours of flight duty, I could not bring myself to notify the hotel about my freezing room.

At the far end of the bedroom, I noticed a deep tub and filled it with hot water. The porcelain, mug-like tub was so tiny that I had to pull my knees to my chest to fit in. The water covered my shoulders, and I finally warmed up. I left the water in the bathtub and climbed into bed, piling all my clothes on top. Within an hour, the hot water in the tub had heated the room.

Our crew had been scheduled for a five-day layover,

and my room problems were fixed the next day. Working for a charter company, we often received numerous days at U.S. airbases. To have the extra days in Tokyo was a blessing, especially before the Christmas season.

The other flight attendants wanted to shop the Ginza area. I wanted to explore Hakone, a high-altitude resort near the base of Mt. Fuji. Early the next morning, I registered with an American tour group and began a ten-hour adventure into the Japanese countryside.

We traveled by both commuter and switchback trains. Our final mode of transportation was a cable car that took us to the snow-covered resort.

Our guide told us, "You can warm up by participating in a hot bath or you can go to a restaurant for black eggs and tea."

He added, "The bath facility does not provide bathing suits."

The tour group chose the restaurant; I chose the hot bath. Boiling eggs in sulfur water created the black-mottled eggs. I didn't mind trying the eggs, but I wanted to experience a traditional Japanese bath. I asked a fellow tourist to buy an egg for me. I could taste it later on the way back to Tokyo.

At the counter in the bath building, a young woman directed me to the second floor and gave me a towel. The smell of sulfur permeated the staircase and hot air filled the dressing room. I hung my clothes on one of the many exposed hooks, noting that my garments were the only ones in the room.

Wrapping the towel around me, I stepped into the bathing room. A row of ten, knee-high faucets lined the nearest wall to my left. In the center sat a shallow swimming pool with steam rising to the glass ceiling. Live plants circled the beige-tiled room, stretching to the high cover above.

With no one else in the sultry room, I felt comfortable with my nudity. I looked at the swimming pool and thought, "What a spot. Swimming uninterrupted laps. How great is this."

I dropped my towel, and with one enormous plunge, I jumped in.

"Yowl!" I screamed. "Hot! Hot!"

The water must have been 120 degrees. I shot from the pool as fast as I could. Jumping up and down, leaping from one foot to the other, I tried to cool my body.

It wasn't a lap pool as I had thought, but a large, scalding bathtub. As I grabbed my towel, I heard laughter coming from behind some palm trees.

I walked to the far end of the pool and peered between the leaves. Below me on another floor were two men and two women frolicking around a second pool, chatting and laughing -- and completely nude. I watched them for a few minutes and then turned away, afraid of being caught staring at their naked cavorting.

Gripping the towel around me, I tottered barefoot to the room's entrance. I turned to the row of faucets, and noticed long-handled cups and a small, tiled trench. Twisting on the first faucet I felt hot water, but nothing like the temperature of the pool. I moved to the next faucet and did the same thing. It was a little hotter than the first. The third faucet was warmer still.

Taking a ladle, I squatted in front of the first faucet and poured water over my body. Slowly, I moved along the line of faucets. Now I understood the procedure. At the last one, the water came out steaming. My body had adjusted to the hot temperature, and I tried the soaking pool again. It was still super hot, but I no longer suffered like a lobster at a clambake.

Wrapping myself back in the towel, I sensed absolute cleanliness and felt wonderful. I dressed and went downstairs to join the others at the nearby restaurant.

"So, how was it?" asked a gray-haired gentleman.

"It was great," I answered, smiling. "You wouldn't believe the experience."

He gave me a local egg to taste. It was black on the outside, but the inside looked just like a normally boiled egg. There was a slight sulfur flavor when I bit into it.

"It had been cooked in the steaming waters created by a volcano fissure," he explained.

Our tour group next took a boat and crossed Lake Ashi. With snow on the ground, the autumn air appeared clear and cool. The lake was a bright blue, and snowcapped Mt. Fuji sparkled in the distance. A postcard photo could not have been better.

"On most days Mt. Fuji is hidden in clouds," our guide informed us. "You're very lucky."

We returned to Tokyo on the revolutionary "Bullet Train," a silver tube traveling at 130 miles per hour. Clean and comfortable with large windows, our trip back took less than an hour and was a perfect end to a fabulous excursion.

Maureen, my roommate for the five-day layover, greeted me on my arrival. She showed me pearls and a camera she had purchased. Each crew member also bought the popular four-foot-high charcoal grill, or *hibachi*. It was shaped like a giant green egg. I added my name to the list, and the hotel called in the extra order.

The next day Maureen and I walked to a nearby neighborhood, exploring the narrow streets lined with small one-story homes. Wind whirled the roadside snow into drifts, some two feet high. As we trudged along, a local resident greeted us.

"Hi. My name is Sumiko. I'm studying English. Can you help me learn?"

After a few minutes of chatting about schools and family, she invited us into her home to meet her mother, Mrs. Hatta. We took off our boots at the front door, put on soft slippers, and walked across straw tatami mats.

The living room/dining area had patio doors that showcased a tiny garden with miniature statues and large stones protruding through the snow. Sitting on pillows around a low table, we could see the garden while we enjoyed some tea. The three of us sat while Mrs. Hatta waited on us.

Their home office converted to a bedroom at night. Sumiko showed us how she pushed the chairs to the side and unfolded a futon (a mat on the floor). The inner wall, from floor to ceiling, was composed of cabinets containing office supplies, sheets, pillows, blankets and a small Shinto shrine.

"Thank you for allowing us into your home," Maureen said, bowing slightly as we started to leave.

"I hope we helped you with your English, Sumiko," I added.

"We are pleased you accepted my invitation," Sumiko said, bowing alongside her mother.

It was all very formal, but truly unique. We remarked about the extraordinary invitation. Although Japanese people are friendly, they are very private.

The other flight attendants appeared jealous of our adventure. Maureen mentioned that we were going to a local restaurant for dinner, instead of dining at the hotel.

She asked, "Would anyone want to join us?"

Julie raised her hand and said, "I will."

The others opted for the comfort and convenience of the hotel, while the three of us bundled up in our uniform coats and wrapped our necks with scarves. As we walked the few blocks to the restaurant, we passed buildings that lined the one-lane thoroughfare. It was more like an alley than a road. With the snow falling and the streetlamps glistening, it looked like an enchanting movie scene.

Julie, Maureen, and I stamped our boots clear of snow and sat by the window in the cafe. Frost covered the windowpanes and reflected the candlelight on our table. The three of us ordered dinner and hot sake, a rice wine that came in small ceramic vessels. Tiny matching cups accompanied each vessel. It wasn't long before we were warm, laughing, and totally relaxed.

On our way back to the hotel, bundled in our coats and scarves, we watched our steamy breath in the cold night air. A gust of wind whipped up the snow as we passed a lighted building. Music and giggling came from a gap in the shutters of a known geisha house. A yellow glow filled a window at least a foot above our heads.

"What's going on in there?" I asked.

"Let's look," Maureen said.

The sake gave us courage. Julie crouched down and laced her gloved fingers together. I stepped onto her hands, and Maureen braced my body. I pulled myself up to the window's ledge. Snow billowed across the sill as I peeked in.

Within a small room sat three teenage girls kneeling in front of three older men. The girls had on white make-up and wore colorful kimonos. The men had their backs to the window, sat cross-legged on cushions, and wore dark suits with white shirts. As two girls played small banjo-type instruments, the third one poured tea into the men's cups. They chatted together, and the young girls bowed their heads, covering their mouths whenever they laughed.

With a little twisting of my body, Julie and Maureen lowered me to the ground.

"What's going on?" they whispered.

"See for yourself," I said and helped lift Julie to the window.

When we lowered her, Maureen took a peek, and then we decided to leave. Our boots crunched on the hard snow as we made our way back to the hotel.

"Can you believe how elaborate their outfits were?" Julie asked.

Their kimonos had vivid orange and red colors with gigantic flower designs. Beads and ornaments dangled from the girls' jet-black hair, forming a dramatic contrast against their white make-up. The flight attendants back at the hotel would be sorry they missed another interesting adventure.

Early the following morning I heard ringing bells outside my hotel room window. Still in my nightclothes, I pushed the curtains aside and peered out. The sweet melody came from a garbage truck. Neighbors had placed their trash on the roadside. They wrapped small bundles in newspapers and tied them with colorful ribbons. It looked like Christmas presents had lined the snow-covered roadway.

The people of Japan are extremely neat and very well organized. They have countless unique customs. I found it an unbelievable experience to have extra days in their country.

While Maureen and I had been exploring, the other crew members engaged in an extravagant shopping spree. When we left Tokyo two days later, the Boeing 707 cargo area was filled with three motorcycles, two rifles and numerous other guns, nine giant hibachis, and many boxes of dishes, lacquerware, silverware, cameras, and stereos.

In our suitcases we brought home pearl jewelry, ivory carvings, happi coats, kimonos, and handmade Western clothes. Friends and relatives would certainly enjoy a special Christmas that year after our crew's lavish shopping binge.

Before our departure, the hotel surprised us with an invitation to a special meal. They knew the fourth Thursday in November was an American holiday. The chef made a traditional Thanksgiving dinner with turkey, mashed potatoes, and pumpkin pie. We were indeed surprised and very appreciative of the effort the hotel and chef made.

Leaving Tokyo meant we crossed the International Date Line when we returned to the United States. Our airline manager in Japan wanted the military passengers to not miss out on Thanksgiving, so he ordered turkey, potatoes, and pie for the soldiers. I love turkey and thought the dinner on board was pretty good. I'm sure the weary combatants were exceptionally happy with the airline meal.

When we refueled in Anchorage we gained a calendar day, and it was Thanksgiving all over again. Local volunteers greeted the G.I.'s with cloth-covered tables piled with turkey, stuffing, gravy, peas, potatoes, and several varieties of pie. The men lined up with the airline crew right behind them. We filled our plates and emptied the tables of all the goodies. Our third Thanksgiving dinner was the best of all.

I called home when we arrived late in the afternoon at Travis Air Force Base. "Don't wait for me," I said. "I won't be home for three more hours."

"Not to worry," Carole answered. "Bob is coming over, and we have a surprise. We postponed Thanksgiving dinner. We'll have it when you get home."

She continued, "We'll have turkey, mashed potatoes, and pumpkin pie…your favorite."

COMING HOME

"Here they come," Janet announced.

We hurried to our assigned positions, standing in our uniforms at the top and bottom ramps of the Boeing 707. Within minutes we would be leaving Vietnam.

"Hi, there, fellows. Welcome aboard," I said, smiling as the G.I.'s raced up the portable stairs.

Our flight from Saigon to Yokota Air Force Base brought tears of joy from our passengers. The military men were on their way home and it was the Fourth of July.

You could feel their sighs of relief as they boarded. Once the plane lifted off the runway, the men erupted in applause and laughter.

Connie and Robin were assigned to the plane's rear section. Marlene worked the back galley while I had the front galley. Janet, a no-nonsense brunette from New York, was the senior flight attendant. She waited on the cockpit and helped with service to those soldiers in the front of the plane.

As soon as the jet leveled out, the cabin crew

changed into yellow smocks. Connie and Robin served orange juice to the men while Marlene and I began preparations for the meal service. More than anything, the men wanted milk with their dinner. They ate every bit of food on the trays and asked for more milk. They ate so quickly and with such gusto I thought they would choke.

Once the meals had been served and the clean up completed, Connie suggested, "Let's put on a skit. We need to thank them for their year in Vietnam."

All the flight attendants agreed to a dancing and singing spectacle. We were proud of them and so grateful that they had survived and were going home.

Robin, a bubbly blond, talked three men out of their khaki hats and shirts. Connie, another beautiful blond, confiscated a pair of lace-up poplin and leather boots.

Singing and dancing.

Marlene (a German blond) joined the two of them and donned one more military shirt and hat. They attached an American flag to the ceiling above the rear galley, and I arrived with my camera to capture the event.

Then our singing began. The three blond flight attendants sang "Caissons Go Rolling Along" as they marched up the aisle from the rear galley, waving napkins and dancing. The men soon joined in.

A rousing chorus of "Yankee Doodle Dandy" followed. Then came a sweet rendition of "America the Beautiful." A few of the men shouted the words, but some of the voices were outstanding.

Their harmony blew us away. They could have been part of a military chorus, crooning for a president's inauguration. By the time we sang "The Star Spangled Banner," there wasn't a dry eye on the plane.

The Fourth of July.

Captain Thomas left the cockpit door open so the flight deck could hear the music. Janet told me the flight crew sang right along with the passengers.

I had left the front of the plane to photograph the singing and dancing in the rear cabin. After we returned the clothes we had borrowed, we told the soldiers how much we appreciated their service to our country. They were truly a wonderful group of men. Before long, most were fast asleep. And we were back to our normal airline duties.

GLOSSARY OF AIRLINE TERMS

Arm and Cross Check: To *arm* is to connect the evacuation slide to the clips at the bottom of exit doors. To *cross check* is to check that the door across the aisle has also been armed and that its chute is now engaged.

Belly: Where baggage and/or freight is generally loaded. This is the area underneath the plane's main cabin. There are usually two main sections, the forward and aft belly compartments. These are pressurized the same as the passenger cabin. The forward belly compartment is used for the transportation of animals and plants. It is temperature and air regulated.

Bidding: Crew members *bid* usually once a month to join a specific crew or to fly to certain places. The *bid* is awarded according to the crew member's seniority.

Bulkhead: The wall between two sections of the airplane.

Bumped: When flying for personal reasons or on a discounted ticket, one could be *bumped* (removed from the flight) if a paying passenger or a person with a higher priority showed up.

Cabin Crew: Those crew members operating in the cabin—a senior flight attendant and four support flight attendants worked Boeing 707 and Douglas DC-8 jets.

Call: *On call* (or on reserve or on standby) meant that crew members had to have their bags packed and be ready to work a flight at a moment's notice. If one were going to be away for more than twelve hours, the Operations Department had to be notified of other telephone numbers. No alcohol could be consumed while on call.

Captain: The *captain* has full responsibility for the aircraft, passengers, and crew from the time the aircraft is loaded at the gate until the termination of the flight. The entire crew is his responsibility (even at layovers) until the crew is broken up by other assignments.

Check Flight: A flight operated for the purpose of testing personnel whether they're cabin or cockpit crew. These are conducted by the airline company and/or FAA check personnel.

Chief Flight Attendant: The person in charge of all flight attendants at an airline.

CPR: Cardiopulmonary resuscitation. Chest compression and artificial breathing performed on an individual in an emergency.

Deadhead: If you are a *deadheading* crew member, you are sometimes paid to fly as a passenger on your company's or on another carrier's airplane. This was used to position crews for future assignments.

Dispatcher: A *dispatcher* gives crew officials direction as to flight destination, layovers, and crew employees. Dispatch is the office where we signed in when reporting for duty, or signed out when returning to home base. Dispatch alerted the scheduling department of any delays or needs for crew or plane changes.

Engineer: The *engineer* sits behind the first officer, facing a panel of electrical switches and various other controls. He must have a mechanical background and is responsible for all the systems of the aircraft.

FAA: Federal Aviation Administration. The *FAA* is responsible for the rules and regulations governing all U.S. airports, the airlines, and their employees.

Ferry: To *ferry* is to fly a plane without passengers or cargo payload to another destination.

First Officer or Co-Pilot: If the captain becomes disabled, the *first officer* assumes complete control of the aircraft, the passengers, and the crew. He sits in the front right seat of the cockpit.

Flight Attendant: A cabin crew member who provides comfort, food, and safety to airline passengers. She is the first responder in case of an inflight health or plane emergency.

Flight Crew: Those employees in the cockpit—Captain, First Officer, Engineer, Navigator, and quite often a Company Check Airman.

Flight Deck: Cockpit and *flight deck* are interchangeable words.

Galley: A *galley* is a small kitchen. One *galley* was located in the front and one was located in the rear on both the Boeing 707 and the Douglas DC-8 jets.

Gate Agent or Ramp Agent: The gate agent meets the plane at arrival and shuts the entrance door before departure. He hands over and receives a manifest and other paperwork.

Go-around: When a pilot has to abort a landing, he initiates a *go-around*. The plane flies back into the air and goes around to make another landing attempt. A go-around usually occurs in bad weather, if the airstrip is blocked, because of tower instructions, or if the plane has incorrect speed and/or altitude.

Gooks, VC, Charlie: Names used to dehumanize the Vietcong and North Vietnamese during the Vietnam War.

Home Base: Oakland was our *home base*. Once we had a sufficient rest period (usually two to five days), we were on call. We had to check in every twelve hours whenever we were away from our regular contact number.

Jet Bridge: The elevated, covered structure between the terminal and the airplane. It is used to protect passengers from the weather and had not yet been invented when I flew.

Jump seat: An extra seat in the cockpit used by check airmen or an observation crew member. The *jump seats* in the front and rear cabin hold two people each. All *jump seats* fold away when not in use.

Layover: A place on line where the crew rests and waits for their upcoming departure flight. *Layovers* were usually a few days. Crews were required to stay at a designated hotel and were on call at all times. A captain's permission was required for any extended time away from the hotel.

Leg: A *leg* is one section of the flight; i.e., Oakland to Tokyo with a refueling stop in Anchorage would employ two *legs* on the journey—Oakland to Anchorage and Anchorage to Tokyo.

Line: The *line*, or the route, the airline flies.

MAC flights: Military Airlift Command.

Manifest: A document including passenger and crew names, cargo details, and the plane's point of departure and destination.

Navigator: The *navigator* sat behind the captain. He worked with charts and estimated times of arrival. His position has been eliminated from modern aircraft.

Operations: Known as *Operations*, the Operations Department supervised, monitored, and coordinated the activities of the airline.

PA: *Public announcement* system or intercom.

Per Diem: A daily pay increment made to compensate for personal expenses (taxis, food, valets, etc.) incurred while on line. We received the same *per diem* amount whether we were in New York City or the Philippines.

Portable Stairs: A stair contraption that needs to be pushed to the plane's doors for passengers to enter or exit. Now they are used mostly with small, regional airplanes.

Pushback: When a plane is ready to leave the terminal and before it is ready to taxi on its own, a *pushback* is required. This is achieved by attaching a tractor to the nose gear with a tow bar and pushing the aircraft back off the gate and out onto a taxiway.

R & R: A military code for "Rest and Recuperation." *R & R* gave military personnel the chance to relax and take a break before returning to war zones.

Reserve: *Reserve*, on call, and stand-by are interchangeable words.

Scheduling: The *Scheduling* Department arranged future flights, planes, and crews. The scheduler called to alert flight crews of upcoming trips.

Senior: The *senior* is the lead flight attendant, the one in charge of all flight attendants on board the plane. She does required paperwork, makes announcements, and regularly reports to the captain. She sits in the forward jump seat next to the telephone and cockpit door.

Seniority: The hired date for a crew member. If two flight attendants were in the same graduating class, the *seniority* goes by date of birth, the oldest having the more senior position. *Seniority* affects one's salary, bidding preferences, and vacation dates.

Space Available: A crew member may fly *space available* on an airline. To accommodate additional passengers or someone with higher priority, the crew member flying *space available* might be bumped off the flight.

Standby: *Standby*, on call, and on reserve are interchangeable words. Regarding ticket purchases, however, *standby* means the same as space available. Although you might have a ticket, you may have to deplane if a paid passenger appears.

USO: United Service Organizations. *USO* is a nonprofit organization that is not a government entity but is sanctioned by the Department of Defense. It provides entertainment and services to the military.

Yoke: The *yoke* or "control column" generally refers to the main flight controls for the airplane. There are two, both for the captain and first officer. They are interconnected and are similar to an automobile's steering wheel. However, they are much more complicated and control a multitude of functions required for flight.

Unions: Before *unions*, flight attendants worked unlimited hours and days. When I began flying, I had low seniority. I once remained on duty for thirty-six hours. Another time I took a sick flight attendant's position in London and instead of flying home, worked another ten days. My thirty-day trip was unusual but not extraordinary.

ACKNOWLEDGEMENTS

I am indebted to all those who have encouraged and helped me through my three years of writing.

In Alphabetical Order:

Cover: Elaine French, Daryl Hunt, and Nancy Strand.

Editing: Al Desetta.

Encouragement: Anyone who listened to my stories and said, "You should write a book." I read chapters to friends and strangers in airplanes, trains, salons, and at the Tellico Village Rover Run Dog Park.

Formatting: Tom Weiland, StarWorks Marketing & Communications.

Marketing: Cindy Chapman Callan and Gabrielle Will Peterson.

Photographs: Provided by Flight Attendants Carla Schulte Reinking and Bobbi Phelps Wolverton.

Proofing: Air Force Navigator Larry Chapman, Virginia Phelps Clemens, Barbara Furlong, Gretchen Gilligan, Aeronautic Instructor Dick Kalman, Buddy Macatee, Susan Church Moore, Flight Attendant Carla Schulte Reinking, Senior Flight Attendant Roxie Sanders, Flight Engineer Sandy Sanders, Captain Jerry Sedik, Bill Sport, Gail Thomasson, Maureen Weber, Flight Attendant Supervisor Jean Wagers-Wiseman, Captain Johnny Wiseman, and Coast Guard Electronics Technician Matthew M. Wolverton.

Reference Consultant: Librarian Jamie Osborn.

Stories: Senior Flight Attendant Ingrid Baehr, Chief Flight Attendant Wayne England, Flight Attendant Ronni Harris, Senior Flight Attendant Helga Komp Hodge, Senior Flight Attendant Rosemarie Haase Paulin and Flight Attendant Carla Schulte Reinking.

Web Page: Lou Miller.

Writing Advice: Spud Hilton, Knoxville Writers' Group, Nick Lyons, Buddy Macatee, and Tellico Writers Inspiration Group.

ABOUT THE AUTHOR

Bobbi Phelps Wolverton, Dubai, 2012

Bobbi Phelps Wolverton grew up in Darien, Connecticut, forty miles from New York City. Following graduation from Pine Manor College and Katharine Gibbs Secretarial School, she was employed as a legal secretary in San Francisco. In 1965 she joined World Airways as an international flight attendant.

In 1967 Bobbi traveled solo around the world and returned to complete her education at the University of California, Berkeley. She then rejoined the charter industry, working for Saturn Airways until 1973.

Bobbi became a professional photographer and copywriter after completing her airline career. From knowledge gained as an employee at Sierra Designs, she started the Angler's Calendar and Catalog Company in 1975. The calendars eventually sold to thirty foreign countries, and in 1993 her business won Exporter of the Year for the State of Idaho (small company category).

Bobbi was a twenty-year member of the Outdoor Writers Association of America, an Arnold Gingrich recipient with the International Federation of Fly Fishers, and a nine-year Idaho board member for The Nature Conservancy. Her volunteer activities also included fundraising for numerous charities, serving as a school board member, and chairing the Trout Festival in Buhl, Idaho.

Behind the Smile is Bobbi's first book. Her second book will describe her eighteen-month backpacking trip around the world, and her third book will portray Bobbi's life as a city girl living on a four-thousand-acre ranch in the middle of nowhere, many miles from Twin Falls, Idaho.

Visit the author's website at www.bobbiphelpswolverton.com

Behind the Smile

Sex, Humor, and Terror

During the Glamour Years of Aviation

By Bobbi Phelps Wolverton

$_____ $14.95   times _____ number of copies.

$_____   9% Tax   ($1.35 each book if mailed to TN).

$_____   U.S.A. Shipping & Handling.   ($2.99 each book).

$_____   Total ($17.94 each book w/o tax). Ck # _____
           Make check out to Village Concepts.

Email: _____

Visa/ MC #: _____

Expiration: _____   3-Digit Code: _____

Mailing address:

Street: _____

City: _____

State: _____   Zip: _____

Email for multiple order discount. No returns allowed.
villageconcepts@charter.net
www.bobbiphelpswolverton.com

Village Concepts, LLC, 124 Chota Shores, Loudon, TN 37774.